J.R. Seeley

**Natural Religion**

J.R. Seeley

**Natural Religion**

ISBN/EAN: 9783743305618

Manufactured in Europe, USA, Canada, Australia, Japa

Cover: Foto ©Thomas Meinert / pixelio.de

Manufactured and distributed by brebook publishing software
(www.brebook.com)

J.R. Seeley

**Natural Religion**

# ATUR

# PREFACE TO THE SECOND EDITION

IT seems not to be clearly understood that this book deals with a strictly limited question. In the first chapter I state that it is my purpose "not to try the question between religion and science but simply to measure how much ground is common to both." As I meant the inquiry to be serious, I thought it essential to take the scientific view frankly at its worst. I therefore make no attempt to show that the negative conclusions so often drawn from modern scientific discoveries are not warranted, but admitting freely for argument's sake all these conclusions, I argue that the total effect of them is not to destroy theology or religion or even Christianity, but in some respects to revive and purify all three. For I maintain that the essential nature of religion is popularly misconceived, and that an accident of it, viz. supernaturalism, is mistaken for its essence.

And in this book I attempt nothing more. It is a matter of course that such an argument should leave on the mind of a supernaturalist a somewhat painful impression, for naturally he wants to see the negations of science refuted rather than to meet with an estimate of the precise amount of destruction caused by them.

I however did think it important to fix the meaning of the word "religion," and to do so before proceeding further, for I found it impossible to handle the subject at all without giving the word a more precise and self-consistent meaning than it has in ordinary parlance. I have therefore written what may be called an essay on the province of religion. I also thought it important that this essay should appear by itself, because I desired that it should receive real attention, and I felt sure that, if it appeared as a mere introduction to a treatise on the burning question of supernaturalism, it would receive no attention whatever.

But if it distresses any one to think that I personally abandon all that the extreme school call in question, certainly he may console himself. I have indeed desired to express the warmest sympathy with all those who advance science, and also the strongest conviction of the essential importance of truly scientific method. It is certainly implied in this, that I have no great respect for the traditional science of theology such as it has come down to us from unscientific times artificially protected against revision. There are also particular theological opinions which this book treats not merely as temporarily out of fashion but as really obsolete, such as the legal or forensic view of the Divine Government, and again that

geration of supernaturalism which crushes the
ent life under the weight of an overwhelming
re.　But in general the negative view is regarded
his book no otherwise than as I find it to be
rded by most of those to whom the book is
cipally addressed, viz. as a fashionable view
cult for the moment to resist, because it seems
ured by great authorities, a view therefore
erning which, however unwillingly, we cannot
asking ourselves the question, What if it should
out to be true?　But if I were asked what I
elf think of it, I should remark that it is not the
test scientific authorities who are so confident in
tion, but rather the inferior men who echo their
ions but who live themselves in the atmosphere
of science but of party controversy; that fashion,
ems to me, is little less influential and little less
meral in opinion than in dress; that it is not on
morrow of great discoveries that we can best
e of their negative effect upon ancient beliefs;
that I am disposed to agree with those who
k that in the end the new views of the Universe
not gratify an extreme party quite so much as is
supposed.
find, however, that some readers have held that
ust be taken to admit whatever in this book I do
undertake to refute, and have drawn the con-
on that I consciously reject Christianity!　Others
understood me to confess that on the questions
ue between religion and science I have nothing

to say, a confession which I never meant to make. That some should consider the book adverse in its effect to Christianity, that is to what they take for Christianity, was a matter of course, but that any one could suppose it was so intended amazes me. Perhaps the misunderstanding has been caused by the condensed style I have adopted. An author has always to decide whether he will write *short* or *long;* and 't is a choice of evils. If he writes long the public will decline to read him; if he, writes short they will misunderstand him.

I have always felt and feel now as much as ever that my ideas are Christian; I am surprised that any one can question it. No doubt when a writer calls himself Christian he uses an expression which may bear a great variety of meanings. Often it means only that he does not intend to quarrel with the religious world, or that he thinks Christianity on the whole a useful and beneficial influence. But when I use it I mean something more and something more definite. What I mean I can hardly hope to explain to those who after reading this book still need an explanation. But I may say in one word that my ideas are *Biblical*, that they are drawn from the Bible at first-hand, and that what fascinates me in the Bible is not a passage here and there, not something which only a scholar or antiquarian can detect in it, but the Bible as a whole, its great plan and unity, and principally the grand poetic anticipation I find in it of modern views concerning history.

# EDITION

A NUMBER of papers bearing the title Natural Religion were contributed by the present writer to *Macmillan's Magazine* at irregular intervals from 1875 to 1878. Upon those papers this work is founded, but it is by no means a reprint of them. About two-thirds of it may be said to be a reprint in respect of substance, though even here correction has been applied throughout, large additions and omissions made, and in some parts the original matter completely recast. The remaining third part is wholly new in substance as well as in style.

The reader must be cautioned not to enter upon this book with the expectation of finding in it anything calculated to promote either orthodoxy or heterodoxy. The author is one of those simpletons who believe that, alike in politics and religion, there are truths outside the region of party debate, and that these truths are more important than the contending parties will easily be induced to believe. In both departments—the reader will discover that to this author they are scarcely two departments,

but almost one and the same—he watches with a
kind of despair the infatuation of party-spirit gradually surrendering the whole area to dispute and
denial, and despising as insipid whatever is not con-
trovertible, until perhaps at last, when the brawl
subsides from mere exhaustion, a third party is
heard proclaiming that when clever men differ so
much and so long, it is evident that nothing can be
known, and possible even that there is nothing to
know.   In religion the evil is far more inveterate
than in politics—and all the greater is the difficulty
of the present attempt ; indeed we see religion suffering veritably the catastrophe of Poland, which found
such a fatal enjoyment in quarrelling, and quarrelled
so long, that a day came at last when there was no
Poland any more, and then the quarrelling ceased.

*May* 1882.

# CONTENTS

## PART I

### CHAPTER I

GOD IN NATURE . . . . . . . 1

### CHAPTER II

THE ABUSE OF THE WORD "ATHEISM" . . . . 24

### CHAPTER III

THE WORDS "THEOLOGY" AND "RELIGION" . . . 43

### CHAPTER IV

THREE KINDS OF RELIGION . . . . . . . 69

### CHAPTER V

NATURAL RELIGION IN PRACTICE . . . . . 86

# PART II

## CHAPTER I

PAGE
RELIGION AND THE WORLD . . . . . . 111

## CHAPTER II

RELIGION AND CULTURE . . . . . . . 131

## CHAPTER III

NATURAL CHRISTIANITY . . . . . . . 150

## CHAPTER IV

NATURAL RELIGION AND THE STATE . . . . . 172

## CHAPTER V

NATURAL RELIGION AND THE CHURCH . . . . 203

## CHAPTER VI

RECAPITULATION . . . . . . . . 226

# PART I

## NATURAL RELIGION

# CHAPTER I

## GOD IN NATURE

WHEN we listen to the newest school of the expounders of science we sometimes hear with surprise phrases which remind us of the peculiar dialect of Christianity. This happens when the subject is learning and learned men. Who does not remember St. Paul's contempt for "the wisdom of the world," for the Greeks to whom the Gospel was foolishness, and how the Apostle's contempt for learning has been echoed wherever Christian feeling has been vigorous, so that even learned Christians have despised their own learning and have taken a pleasure in placing themselves on a level with the ignorant? Who does not know how at the same time Christianity has contrasted the learning which it contemns with another kind of knowledge which it prizes infinitely? Wealth, power, everything that is counted desirable, Christians despise in comparison with a certain kind of knowledge. It is among these things comparatively despicable that they class what is commonly called learning. They despise it not *as* learning, but as learning comparatively worthless in quality, a counterfeit of the true learning which it is happiness and salvation to possess.

B

Now in this respect scientific men now hold the very same language.  They resemble Christians in treating with great contempt what goes by the name of learning and philosophy, in comparison with another sort of wisdom which they believe themselves to possess.  In praise of knowledge they grow eloquent, and use language of scriptural elevation.  It is their unceasing cry that all good is to be expected from the increase of true knowledge ; that the happiness both of the race and individuals depends upon the advance of real science, and the application of it to human life.  Yet they have a contempt for learning, which is just as Christian in its tone as their love for knowledge.  " Erudition " and " philosophy " are terms of contempt in their mouths.  They denounce the former as a busy idleness, and the latter as a sham wisdom, consisting mainly of empty words, and offering solutions either imaginary or unintelligible of problems which are either imaginary or unintelligible themselves. All members of the modern school are, it is true, not equally plain-spoken ; some will profess to admire scholarship and erudition, speaking of it as a graceful accomplishment ; and it is only in unguarded moments that they betray their conviction that it is nothing more ; but others proclaim it loudly, and a few even wish to bring public opinion to bear upon the matter, so as to suppress as an immorality the acquiring of useless knowledge.

Thus the old religious school, and that new school whose convictions we see now gradually acquiring the character of a religion, agree in combining a passionate love for what they believe true knowledge with a contempt for so-called learning and philosophy.  The common enemy of both is what the one school calls, and the other might well call, "the wisdom of the world." But though agreeing so far, these two schools hate their common enemy much less than they hate each other. For each regards the "true wisdom" of the other as worse and more mischievous than the wisdom of the world which each rejects. To the scientific school the Christian "hidden wisdom" is a mystical superstition, compared with which "learning and philosophy" are science itself. To the Christian, modern science is a darkness compared with which the science that St. Paul rejected might almost be called Christianity.

Nothing is so terrible as this clashing of opposite religions. Differences on subjects of the first importance are always painful, but the direct shock of contrary enthusiasms has something appalling about it. That one man's highest truth should be another man's deadliest falsehood ; that one man should be ready to die in disinterested self-devotion for a cause which another man is equally ready to oppose at the sacrifice of his life ; this is a horror which is none the less horrible because it has often been witnessed on our perplexed planet. But often it has been perceived, long after the conflict was over, that there had been misapprehension, that the difference of opinion was not really anything like so complete as it seemed. Nay, it has often happened that a later generation has seen the difference to be very small indeed, and has wondered that so much could have been made of it. In such cases the mind is relieved of that fancy of a radical discord in human nature. We see that self-devotions have not really clashed in such fell antagonism. We recognise that self-devotion may be alloyed with less noble feelings, with some that are blamable and some that are even ludicrous, with mere pugnacity, with the passion of gratifying self-importance, with the half noble pleasure that there is in fighting, and the ignoble pleasure that there is in giving pain.

It would certainly be hard enough to show that the present strife between Christianity and Science is one in which insignificant differences are magnified by the imagination of the combatants. The question is nothing less than this, whether we are to regard the grave with assured hope, and the ties between human beings as indissoluble by death ; or, on the other hand, to dismiss the hope of a future life as too doubtful to be worth considering, even if not absolutely chimerical. No reasoning can make such a difference into a small one. But even where the differences are so great, it may still be worth while to call attention to the points of agreement. If there is some truth, however small, upon which all can agree, then there is some action upon which all can unite ; and who can tell how much may be done by anything so rare as absolute unanimity? Moreover, if we look below the surface of controversy, we shall commonly find more agreement and less disagreement than we had expected. Agreement is slow of speech and attracts little notice, disagreement has always plenty to say for itself. Agreement utters chiefly platitudes and truisms. And yet, though platitudes and truisms do not work up into interesting books, if our object is to accomplish something for human life, we shall scarcely find any truth serviceable that has not been rubbed into a truism, and scarcely any maxim that has not been worn into a platitude. Let the attempt then be made for once to apply this principle in the greatest and most radical of all controversies. Let us put religion by the side of science in its latest most aggressive form, with the view not of trying the question between them, but simply of measuring how much ground is common to both. In their tone, in their attitude towards philosophy and learning there seems some resemblance. Let us examine this resemblance more closely.

We are all familiar with the language used by Christians in disparagement of learning. God, they say, has revealed to men all that is essential for them to know. By the side of revealed knowledge what the human intellect can discover for itself is of little importance. If it seem to clash with revelation it is mischievous; if not, it may be useful in a subordinate degree. But at the best it is contemptible by the side of the "one thing needful"; and the greatest discoverer that ever lived is a trifler compared with the most simple-minded Christian who has studied to fulfil the requirements of the Gospel.

There is indeed a true erudition and a true philosophy, the subject of which is God's revelation itself. Scholars, profoundly read in the sources of theology, whether they be supposed to be the Bible or Christian Antiquity, philosophers who have made the Christian revelation their basis, or have collected and elucidated the evidences of it—these are truly wise, and escape the censure of frivolity under which secular learning lies; but even these, illustrious and venerable as they may be, will acknowledge that there is a wisdom beyond their own, which the humblest Christian may possess, the wisdom of simple belief and love.

We are less familiar as yet with the invectives of scientific men against what has long passed for learning and philosophy in the world. Different sections of the scientific school bring the accusation in different language. Yet the same feeling, the same strong and contemptuous conviction, pervades the whole school. What they assail seems to be, in two words, knowledge based on authority, and knowledge wanting an inductive basis.

That the utterances of great and famous philosophers are to be taken as truth, that in philosophy as in the civil law, the *responsa prudentum* have a binding force, has been accepted in some departments of knowledge up to the present day. Long after the authority of Aristotle had been shaken new thinkers were allowed to occupy a similar place in some branches, and from Descartes to Hegel a sort of monarchical rule has prevailed in metaphysics. Science as distinguished from philosophy has always been more republican. Not that it refuses to reverence superior minds, not perhaps that it is altogether incapable of yielding to the temptation of trusting a particular authority for a while too much, or following a temporary fashion. But as a general rule it rejects as a superstition the notion that the most superior mind is at all infallible; it dissents without scruple from those whom it reverences most; and on the other hand the most eminent members of it encourage this freedom, are well pleased to be contradicted, and avoid assuming an oracular style as a mark of charlatanry. We see now the régime of science established in philosophy also; the autocracy of Hegel comes to an end, not by the accession of a new monarch, but rather by the proclamation of a republic in German philosophy.

It is a change of system in the intellectual world, by which much established doctrine is branded with the mark of spuriousness. In theology, metaphysics, moral and political philosophy, history, the principle of authority has reigned hitherto with more or less exclusiveness, and the repudiation of it makes a revolution in those departments of knowledge. Authoritative treatises are consigned to oblivion, ancient controversies cease, the whole store of learning hived up in many capacious memories becomes worthless. The change throws discredit at the same time upon the very name of erudition ; not as such, for there is a kind of erudition much appreciated by the scientific school ; but because erudition, as hitherto understood, has commonly gone along with, has in a great degree grown out of, an excessive reverence for the opinions of famous men. All that part of erudition, in particular, which may be called in a word "commentatorship," begins to seem superstitious and childish, when the general estimate of human wisdom so decidedly sinks.

But the more important change is in the extension of the *methods* of physical science to the whole domain of knowledge. While one part of the "wisdom of the world" has been discredited as resting solely on authority, another large division of it is now rejected as resting on insufficient induction, and another as resting on groundless assumptions, disguised under the name of necessary truths, truths of the reason, truths given in consciousness, etc. No one needs to be told what havoc this physical method is making with received systems, and it produces a sceptical disposition of mind towards primary principles which have been thought to lie deeper than *all* systems. Those current abstractions, which make up all the morality and all the philosophy of most people, have been brought under suspicion. Mind and matter, duties and rights, morality and expediency, honour and interest, virtue and vice,—all these words, which seemed once to express elementary and certain realities, now strike us as just the words which, thrown into the scientific crucible, might dissolve at once. It is thus not merely philosophy which is discredited, but just that homely and popular wisdom by which common life is guided. This too, it appears, instead of being the sterling product of plain experience, is the overflow of an immature philosophy, the redundance of the uncontrolled speculations of thinkers who were unacquainted with scientific method.

This second change leads to self-distrust, as the first led to distrust of other men. As we learn not to take our truth at second-hand from other thinkers, so we learn that we must not take it, if the expression may be used, from ourselves. Truth is not what *we* think, any more than it is what famous men have thought. That which irresistibly strikes us as true, that which seems self-evident, that which commends itself to us, may nevertheless, we learn, not be true at all. It is not enough to judge for ourselves, to examine the facts independently. We must examine the facts according to a rigorous method, which has been elaborated by a long series of investigators, and without which neither candour nor impartiality would save us either from seeing wrong, or from receiving unsound evidence, or from generalising too fast, or from allowing some delusive name to come between us and the reality. Distrust of others, distrust of ourselves—if the first of these two factors of the scientific

spirit were separated from the second, the result would be
mere self-conceit, mere irreverence.   As it is, the scientific
spirit is simply a jealous watchfulness against that tendency
of human nature to read itself into the Universe, which is
both natural to each individual and may mislead the very
greatest investigators, and which can only be controlled by
rigorously adhering to a fixed process, and rigidly verifying
the work of others by the same.

Such untested knowledge might very fitly be called by
the name which Christianity uses.   It might be called
"human knowledge," or "the wisdom of the world."   For
the difference between it and genuine knowledge is just this,
that it is adulterated by a human element.   It is not the
result of a contact between the universe and the naked
human intelligence.   The perceiving mind has mixed itself
up with the thing perceived, and not merely in the way in
which it always must, in the way which constitutes cognition,
but in quite other and arbitrary ways, by wishes, by prejudices, by crotchets, by dreams.   Such humanised views
of the Universe have a peculiar though cheap attractiveness.
They naturally please the human mind, because, in fact,
they were expressly contrived to do so.   They adapt themselves readily to rhetoric and poetry, because, in fact, they
*are* rhetoric and poetry in disguise.   To reject them is to
mortify human nature ; it is an act of vigorous asceticism.   It
is to renounce the world as truly as the Christian does when
he protests against fashionable vices.   It is to reject a
pleasant thing on the ground that it is insincere ; that it is
not in fact what it professes to be.   The moral attitude of
the man who does it is just such as Hebrew prophets assumed

towards the flattering and lying court-prophets of their days;
just such as the earliest Christianity assumed towards
Pharisaism; just such as Luther and Knox assumed towards
the secularised Church of the later Middle Age. It is an
attitude of indignant sincerity, an attitude marking an inward
determination to accept the truth of the Universe, however
disagreeable, and not to allow it to be adulterated and
drugged, so as to suit our human feebleness. If we cannot
produce from the Scriptures of our religion texts directly
sanctioning it, this is because the particular problem was not
presented in ancient times to the Jewish nation. Those
Scriptures are full of passages expressing in poetic forms and
in language suited to another age the spirit of modern science.
Notably, the book of Job, not in occasional passages only,
but as its main object and drift, contrasts the conventional,
and, as it were, orthodox view of the Universe, with the
view which those obtain who are prepared to face its awfulness directly.

Thus the religious view and the scientific view of the
Universe, which are thought to be so opposite, agree in this
important point. Both protest earnestly against human
wisdom. Both wait for a message which is to come to them
from without. Religion says, "Let man be silent, and listen
when God speaks." Science says, "Let us interrogate
Nature, and let us be sure that the answer we get is really
Nature's, and not a mere echo of our own voice." Now
whether or not religion and science agree in what they recommend, it is evident that they agree in what they denounce.
They agree in denouncing that pride of the human intellect
which supposes it knows everything, which is not passive

enough in the presence of reality, but deceives itself with pompous words instead of things, and with flattering eloquence instead of sober truth.

Here, however, it will be said, the agreement between religion and science ends, and even this agreement is only apparent. Science protests against the idols or delusions of the human intellect, in order that it may substitute for them the reality of Nature; religion sacrifices all those idols to the greatest of them all, which is God. For what is God— so the argument runs—but a hypothesis, which religious men have mistaken for a demonstrated reality? And is it not precisely against such premature hypotheses that science most strenuously protests? That a Personal Will is the cause of the Universe—this might stand very well as a hypothesis to work with, until facts should either confirm it, or force it to give way to another either different or at least modified. That this Personal Will is benevolent, and is shown to be so by the facts of the Universe, which evince a providential care for man and other animals—this is just one of those plausibilities, which passed muster before scientific method was understood—but modern science rejects it as unproved. Modern science holds that there may be design in the Universe, but that to penetrate the design is, and probably always will be, beyond the power of the human understanding. That this Personal Will has on particular occasions revealed itself by breaking through the customary order of the Universe, and performing what are called miracles—this—it is said—is one of those legends of which histories were full, until a stricter view of evidence was introduced, and the modern critical spirit sifted thoroughly the annals of the world. But if modern science be right in these opinions, the very notion of God seems to be removed altogether from the domain of practical life. So long as God appeared certainly to exist, He necessarily eclipsed and reduced to insignificance all other existences. So long as it was held possible to discover His will and mind, all other inquiries might reasonably be pronounced frivolous. But all is changed as soon as we begin to regard His existence as a mere hypothesis, and His will as inscrutable and beyond the reach of the human understanding. Not only is all changed, but all is reversed. Instead of being the one important question, God's will now becomes the one *un*important question because the one question which it is essentially impossible to answer. Whereas before we might charge men with frivolity who neglected this inquiry for inquiries the most important in themselves, now we may pronounce the shallowest dilettante, the most laboriously idle antiquary, a solid and sensible man compared to the theologian. They pursue, to be sure, very minute objects, but they do or may attain them ; the theologian attempts an impossibility—he is like the child who tries to reach the beginning of the rainbow.

It would appear, then, that that which I have called "human wisdom," and which is the butt at the same time of theology and science, is so because it is a kind of middle party between two mortally hostile factions. It is like the Girondins between the Royalists and the Jacobins ; both may oppose, and may even in a particular case combine to oppose it, and yet they may feel not the slightest sympathy with each other. And the middle party once crushed, there will follow no reconciliation, but a mortal contest between the extremes.

Is this so or is it otherwise? The question is whether the statement given above of the theological view of the Universe is exhaustive or not? Is it all summed up in the three propositions that a Personal Will is the cause of the Universe, that that Will is perfectly benevolent, that that Will has sometimes interfered by miracles with the order of the Universe? If these propositions exhaust it, and science throws discredit upon all of them, evidently theology and science are irreconcilable, and the contest between them must end in the destruction of one or the other.

It may be remarked, in the first place, that these propositions are not so much an abstract of theology as of the particular theology now current. That God is perfectly benevolent is a maxim of popular Christianity, and it may be supported by Biblical texts. But it is not necessary to theology or religion as such. Many nations have believed in gods of mixed or positively malignant character. Other nations have indeed ascribed to their deities all the admirable qualities they could conceive, but benevolence was not one of these. They have believed in gods that were beautiful, powerful, immortal, happy, but not benevolent. It may even be said that the Bible and Christianity itself have not uniformly represented God as perfectly benevolent. In the Old Testament He is described as just, but at the same time terrible and pitiless against the wicked and even the children of the wicked ; and at least one form of modern Christianity, Calvinism, takes a view of the divine character which it is impossible to reconcile with infinite benevolence.

Moreover, if almost all theologies have introduced what we should describe as miracle, yet it would be very incorrect to class many of them in this respect with that current view of Christianity which represents God as demonstrating His existence by occasional interruptions of the order, otherwise invariable, of Nature. Probably, in the majority of theologies, no other law of nature, except the will of God, is recognised; miracle when it is introduced is not regarded as breaking through any order; the very notion implied in the word "supernatural" is unacknowledged; miraculous occurrences are not distinguished from ordinary ones, except as being rarer, and are not distinguished from rare occurrences at all. To an ancient Jew probably an earthquake and the staying of the sun on Gibeon were occurrences of precisely the same character, and not distinguished as they are in our minds, the one as rare but natural, the other as supernatural and miraculous. All that was miraculous might have been removed from the creed of an ancient Jew without shaking his theology.

Two out of the three propositions then are not necessary to the theological view of the Universe. But surely the third is. Surely all theology implies that a Personal Will is the cause of the Universe. Well, but how? In the first place it is a very shallow view of theologies which represents them as having in all cases sprung from speculation about causes. True that we can trace this speculation in our own religion. The phenomena of the world are accounted for very manifestly in the book of Genesis by the fiat of a Personal Will. But this is not at all an invariable character of theology. The *Deity of a thing* is often regarded in theologies not at all as the cause of it, but in quite another way, perhaps I might say as the *unity* of it. No one has ever supposed that the Greeks regarded Poseidon as the *cause* of the sea. Athena may have been suggested to them by the sky, but she is not the *cause* of the sky. And it would be easy to conceive a theology which did not occupy itself at all with causes, but which at the same time conceived the separate phenomena of the Universe, or the Universe itself altogether *personally*.

"Yes, personally! Here then at any rate we have the invariable characteristic of theology, namely, in the use it makes of personality. Not necessarily as a cause, but in some way as an explanation or at least as a help to conception, theologies introduce personality where science sees only impersonal force." Even this statement is loose enough. Personality entire has never been attributed in any theology to deities. Personality, as we know it, involves mortality. Deities are usually supposed immortal. Personality involves a body. The highest theologies have declared God to be incorporeal. May we then fall back upon the will and say, Theologies attribute to deities a *will* like that of human beings? But again the highest theologies assert that the Divine Will is high above the human ; that there is "no searching" of it ; "that as the heaven is high above the earth, so are His ways than our ways, and His thoughts than our thoughts."

If the possibility of miracles were entirely given up, and the order of nature decided to be as invariable as science inclines to consider it ; if all the appearances of benevolent design in the Universe were explained away, it might be

true that the belief in God would cease to be consoling.
Instead of being a spring of life and activity, it might—I am
not now saying it would—become a depressing and overwhelming influence. And this, no doubt, is what people
mean when they identify, as they commonly do, the belief
in God with belief in an overruling Benevolence and in the
supernatural. They mean to say, not exactly that the
belief in God *is* necessarily this, but that to be in any way
useful or beneficial it must necessarily be this. But for my
present purpose it is important to distinguish between the
God in whom ordinary people at the present day believe
and a God of another character in whom they might conceivably believe. I desire to insist upon the point that
when science speaks of God as a myth or a hypothesis, and
declares the existence of God to be doubtful and destined
always to remain doubtful, it is speaking of a particular conception of God, of God conceived as benevolent, as outside
of nature, as personal, as the cause of phenomena. Do
these attributes of benevolence, personality, etc., exhaust the
idea of God? Are they—not merely the most important,
the most consoling of His attributes, but—the only ones?
By denying them do we cease not merely to be orthodox
Christians but to be theists?

Science opposes to God Nature. When it denies God
it denies the existence of any power beyond or superior to
Nature; and it may deny at the same time anything like a
*cause* of Nature. It believes in certain laws of coexistence
and sequence in phenomena, and in denying God it means
to deny that anything further can be known. God and
Nature then express notions which are different in an

important particular. But it is evident enough that these notions are not the opposites that controversy would represent them to be. On the contrary, they coincide up to a certain point. Those who believe in Nature may deny God, but those who believe in God, believe, as a matter of course, in Nature also, since God includes Nature, as the whole includes the part. It is no doubt fashionable to represent theology as disregarding Nature, as passing by the laws which govern the Universe, and occupying itself solely with occasional suspensions of them, or with ulterior, inscrutable causes. But this conception of theology is derived from a partial view of it. It answers well enough to a modern phase into which theology has passed since it was expelled from the domain of Nature by the rival and victorious method of physical science. To the older theologies it is wholly inapplicable. They occupied themselves quite as much with laws as with causes; so far from being opposed to science, they were in fact themselves science in a rudimentary form; so far from neglecting the natural for the supernatural, they scarcely recognised any distinction between them. The true object of theology at the beginning was to throw light upon natural laws; it used no doubt a crude method, and in some cases it attempted problems which modern science calls insoluble. Then, when a new method was introduced, theology stuck obstinately to its old one, and when the new method proved itself successful, theology gradually withdrew into those domains where as yet the old method was not threatened, and might still reign without opposition. Thus it began to be supposed that law appertained to science, and suspension of law or miracle to theology; that the one was concerned with Nature, and the other with that which was above Nature. Gradually the name of God began to be associated with the supernatural, until scientific men began to say they had nothing to do with God, and theologians to find something alien to them in the word Nature.

Yet theology can never go further than this in repudiating Nature. It can never deny that Nature is an ordinance of God ; it can never question that the laws of Nature are among the laws of God. It may indeed treat them as His less important laws, or as a revelation of Him which is not precisely the revelation we want. But it cannot and does not deny that Nature too is a revelation of God; it ought not to deny that there is a theology which may be called natural, and which does not consist in a collection of the evidences of benevolent design in the Universe, but in a true deduction of the laws which govern the Universe, whatever those laws may be, and whatever they may seem to indicate concerning the character of God.

But if, on the one hand, the study of Nature be one part of the study of God, is it not true, on the other, that he who believes only in Nature is a theist, and has a theology ? Men slide easily from the most momentous controversies into the most contemptible logomachies. If we will look at things, and not merely at words, we shall soon see that the scientific man has a theology and a God, a most impressive theology, and a most awful and glorious God. I say that man believes in a God who feels himself in the presence of a Power which is not himself and is immeasurably above himself, a Power in the contemplation of which he is absorbed, in the knowledge of which he finds safety and happiness. And such now is Nature to the scientific man. I do not now say that it is good or satisfying to worship such a God, but I say that no class of men since the world began have ever more truly believed in a God, or more ardently, or with more conviction, worshipped Him. Comparing their religion in its fresh youth to the present confused forms of Christianity, I think a bystander would say that though Christianity had in it something far higher and deeper and more ennobling, yet the average scientific man worships just at present a more awful, and, as it were, a greater Deity than the average Christian. In so many Christians the idea of God has been degraded by childish and little-minded teaching; the Eternal and the Infinite and the All-embracing has been represented as the head of the clerical interest, as a sort of clergyman, as a sort of schoolmaster, as a sort of philanthropist. But the scientific man *knows* Him to be eternal; in astronomy, in geology, he becomes familiar with the countless millenniums of His lifetime. The scientific man strains his mind actually to realise God's infinity. As far off as the fixed stars he traces Him, "distance inexpressible by numbers that have name." Meanwhile, to the theologian, infinity and eternity are very much of empty words when applied to the Object of his worship. He does not realise them in actual facts and definite computations.

But it is not merely because he realises a stupendous Power that I call the scientific man a theist. A true theist should recognise his Deity as giving him the law to which his life ought to be conformed. Now here it is that the

resemblance of modern science to theology comes out most
manifestly.  There is no stronger conviction in this age
than the conviction of the scientific man, that all happiness
depends upon the knowledge of the laws of Nature, and the
careful adaptation of human life to them.  Of this I have
spoken before.  Luther and Calvin were not more jealous
of the Church tradition that had obscured the true word of
God in the Scriptures than the modern man of science is
of the metaphysics and conventional philosophy that have
beguiled men away from Nature and her laws.  They want
to remodel all education, all preaching, so that the laws of
Nature may become known to every man, and that every
one may be in a condition to find his happiness in obeying
them.   They chafe at the notion of men studying anything
else.   They behave towards those who do not know Nature
with the same sort of impatient insolence with which a
Christian behaved towards the worshippers of the Emperor
or a Mohammedan towards idolaters.   As I sympathise very
partially with the Mohammedan, and not quite perfectly
with the early Christian, so I find the modern scientific zeal
sometimes narrow and fanatical; but I recognise that it is
zeal of the same kind as theirs, that, like theirs, it is theological.

An infinite Power will inspire awe and an anxious desire
to avoid a collision with it.   But such awe and fear, it may
be said, do not constitute worship; worship implies admiration, and something which may be called love.   Now it is
true that the scientific man cannot feel for Nature such love
as a pious mind may feel for the God of Christians.   The
highest love is inspired by love, or by justice and goodness,

and of these qualities science as yet discerns little or nothing in Nature. But a very genuine love, though of a lower kind, is felt by the contemplator of Nature. Nature, even if we hesitate to call it good, is infinitely interesting, infinitely beautiful. He who studies it has continually the exquisite pleasure of discerning or half discerning and divining *laws ;* regularities glimmer through an appearance of confusion ; analogies between phenomena of a different order suggest themselves and set the imagination in motion ; the mind is haunted with the sense of a vast unity not yet discoverable or nameable. There is food for contemplation which never runs short ; you gaze at an object which is always growing clearer, and yet always, in the very act of growing clearer, presenting new mysteries. And this arresting and absorbing spectacle, so fascinating by its variety, is at the same time overwhelming by its greatness ; so that those who have devoted their lives to the contemplation scarcely ever fail to testify to the endless delight it gives them, and also to the overpowering awe with which from time to time it surprises them.

There is one more feeling which a worshipper should have for his Deity, a sense of personal connexion, and, as it were, relationship. The last verse of a hymn of praise is very appropriately this—" For this God is *our* God for ever and ever ; He will be our guide even unto death." This feeling, too, the worshipper of Nature has. He cannot separate himself from that which he contemplates. Though he has the power of gazing upon it as something outside himself, yet he knows himself to be a part of it. The same laws whose operations he watches in the Universe he may

study in his own body.  Heat and light and gravitation
govern himself as they govern plants and heavenly bodies.
"In Him," may the worshipper of this Deity say with
intimate conviction, "in Him we live and move and have
our being."  When men whose minds are possessed with a
thought like this, and whose lives are devoted to such a
contemplation, say, "As for God, we know nothing of Him;
science knows nothing of Him; it is a name belonging to
an extinct system of philosophy;" I think they are playing
with words.  By what name they call the object of their
contemplation is in itself a matter of little importance.
Whether they say God, or prefer to say Nature, the important thing is that their minds are filled with the sense of a
Power to all appearance infinite and eternal, a Power to
which their own being is inseparably connected, in the
knowledge of whose ways alone is safety and wellbeing, in
the contemplation of which they find a beatific vision.

Well! this God is also the God of Christians.  That the
God of Christians is something more does not affect this
fact.  Nature, according to all systems of Christian theology,
is God's ordinance.  Whether with science you stop short
at Nature, or with Christianity believe in a God who is the
author of Nature, in either case Nature is divine, for it is
either God or the work of God.  This whole domain is
common to science and theology.  When theology says, Let
us give up the wisdom of men and listen to the voice of
God, and when science says, Let us give up human authority
and hollow *a priori* knowledge and let us listen to Nature,
they are agreed to the whole extent of the narrower proposition, *i.e.* theology ought to admit all that science says,

though science admits only a part of what theology says. Theology cannot say the laws of Nature are not divine ; all it can say is, they are not the most important of the divine laws. Perhaps not, but they gain an importance from the fact that they are laws upon which all can agree. Making the largest allowance for discoveries about which science may be too confident, there remains a vast mass of natural knowledge which no one questions. This to the Christian is so much knowledge about God, and he ought to exult quite as much as the man of science in the rigorous method by which it has been separated from the human prejudice and hasty ingenuity and delusive rhetoric or poetry, which might have adulterated it. By this means we have been enabled to hear a voice which is unmistakably God's. And if it seems to be God speaking about matters not the most important, still perhaps it may be as well to listen. So much, at least, reverence would dictate ; and if it did not, the urgent necessity for more agreement on fundamental questions would dictate it imperiously.

# CHAPTER II

I HAVE suggested the thought of a God revealed in Nature, not by any means because such a view of God seems to me satisfactory, or worthy to replace the Christian view, or even as a commencement from which we must rise by logical necessity to the Christian view. I have suggested it because this is the God Whom the present age actually does, and, in spite of all opposition, certainly will worship, also because this aspect of God is common to all theologies, however much in some it may be slighted or depreciated, and lastly, because I do not believe that any theology can be real or satisfying that does not make it prominent as well as admit it. I can conceive no religion as satisfactory that falls short of Christianity, but, on the other hand, I cannot believe any religion to be healthy that does not start from Nature-worship. It is in the free and instinctive admiration of human beings for the glory of heaven, earth and sea, that religion—so far as religion is the name of a good and healthy thing—begins, and I cannot imagine but as morbid a religion which has ceased to admire them.

But many religious men will probably think that not

much is to be hoped from dwelling on this subject. "We know very well that the Universe is glorious, but when you have said that, there is an end of the matter. We want to make atheists believe in God, and you do it not by changing their minds, but by changing the meaning of the word God. It is not a verbal controversy that rages between atheists and Christians; it is the great controversy of the age. Two opposite theories of the Universe are in conflict. On the one side is the greatest of all affirmations, on the other the most fatal of all negations. There never yet was a controversy which was not trivial in comparison with this. It is cruel trifling to speak of compromise, it is waste of time to draw verbal distinctions. Let atheism be atheism, and 'darkness keep her raven gloss'! Away with the plausible definitions which would make it impossible for any rational being ever to be an atheist!"

Now why should we be so wilful as to forget that the error of monstrously overestimating doctrinal differences has been all along the plague of theology? There can be no greater mistake than to measure the real importance of a dispute by the excitement of the disputants. It has often been remarked of theological controversies, that they are never conducted more bitterly than when the difference between the rival doctrines is very small. This is nearly correct, but not quite. If you want to see the true white heat of controversial passion, if you want to see men fling away the very thought of reconciliation, and close in internecine conflict, you should look at controversialists who *do not differ at all*, but who have adopted different words to express the same opinion.

In the controversy which now fills the world and seems not unlikely to give a lurid tinge to the setting of the nineteenth century, there is surely a fair proportion of the old misconception and bewilderment.  The real issue is no doubt a great one, but it is not so great as the issue between theism and atheism.  That a party calls itself atheistic matters little; when did any party name itself accurately?  These so-called atheists do not always appear to be divided from plain people by the whole diameter.  Some of them are so, but others are not so.  This must be because they have been misnamed.

An atheist in the proper sense of the word is not a man who disbelieves in the goodness of God, or in His distinctness from Nature, or in His personality.  These disbeliefs may be as serious in their way as atheism, but they are different.  Atheism is a disbelief in the *existence* of God— that is, a disbelief in *any* regularity in the Universe to which a man must conform himself under penalties.  Such a disbelief is speculatively monstrous; it is a kind of mental deficiency or perversion, but so commonly are the false views which lead to immoral action.

There is an atheism which is a mere speculative crotchet, and there is an atheism which is a great moral disease.  Let me illustrate the latter, which is the real atheism, by some specimens.

The purest form of such real atheism might be called by the general name of *wilfulness*.  All human activity is a transaction with Nature.  It is the arrangement of a compromise between what we want on the one hand, and what Nature has decreed on the other.  Something of our own wishes we have almost always to give up; but by carefully considering the power outside ourselves, the necessity that conditions all our actions, we may make better terms than we could otherwise, and reduce to a minimum what we are obliged to renounce. Now we may either underrate or over-rate the force of our own wills. The first is the extravagance of theism; it is that fatalism which steals so naturally upon those who have dwelt much upon the thought of God, which is said to paralyse, for example, the whole soul of the Mussul-man. But the opposite mistake is a deficiency of theism; a touch of it often marks the hero, but the fulness of it is that kind of blind infatuation which poets have represented under the image of the giants who tried to storm heaven. Not to recognise anything but your own will, to fancy any-thing within your reach if you only will strongly enough, to acknowledge no superior Power outside yourself which must be considered and in some way propitiated if you would succeed in any undertaking; this is complete wilfulness, or, in other words, pure atheism. It may also be called childish-ness, for the child naturally discovers the force within it sooner than the resisting necessity outside. Not without a few falls in the wrestle with Nature do we learn the limits of our own power and the pitiless immensity of the power that is not ours. But there are many who cannot learn this lesson even from experience, who forget every defeat they suffer, and always refuse to see any power in the Universe but their own wills. Sometimes, indeed, they discover their mistake too late. Many barbarous races are in this condi-tion. In their childishness they have engaged themselves in a direct conflict with Nature. Instead of negotiating with her, they have declared a blind war. They have adopted habits which they gradually discover to be leading them to destruction; but they discover it too late and when they are too deeply compromised. Then we see the despair of the atheistic nation, and its wild struggles as it feels itself caught in the whirlpool; then, a little later, we find that no such nation exists, and on the map its seat begins to be covered with names belonging to another language. Less extreme and unredeemed, the same Titanism may sometimes be remarked in races called civilised. Races might be named that are undergoing punishments little less severe for this insensate atheism. "Sedet æternumque sedebit," that un-happy Poland, not indeed extinguished but partitioned, and every thirty years decimated anew. She expiates the crime of atheistic wilfulness, the fatal pleasure of unbounded individual liberty, which rose up against the very nature of things. And other nations we know that expect all successes from the mere blind fury of willing, that declare the word impossible unknown to their language. They colour their infatuation sometimes with the name of self-sacrifice, and fancy they can change the divine laws by offering up them-selves as victims to their own vanity; they "fling themselves against the bars of fate"; they die in theatrical attitudes, and little know how "the abyss is wreathed in scorn" of such cheap martyrdom.

A wrong belief about God, however fatal it may be, is not atheism. Mr. Buckle tried to show that the Spanish empire fell through a false conception of the order of the Universe; and it seems clear that the rigid Catholic view of the world is dangerous in this age to every nation that adopts it. These are the effects of false theology. But there is a state of mind which, though very far removed from the wilfulness I have been describing, and often accompanied with a strong and anxious religiousness, may nevertheless be practically regarded as a form of atheism. It is the state of those minds which, fully believing in an order of the Universe, yet have such a poor and paltry conception of it that they might almost as well have none at all.

Men are sometimes led to this state by a very reasonable and excusable process of thought. Naturally modest and distrustful of their own powers, they despair of understanding the order of the Universe; they do not presume to attempt to understand it. Wisely distrustful of any knowledge that is not precise, they avert their eyes instinctively from everything which cannot be made the subject of such knowledge. In all their transactions with Nature, to use my former phrase, they make it a rule to be unambitious. They aim at objects very definite and very near. Whatever they gain they make it a rule not to expose to any further risk. They avoid, as it were, meeting the Universe in front, and endeavour to overcome it in detail. For its immediate purpose this plan is the best that can be pursued. If in all our actions we allowed ourselves to remember the greatness of the power with which we have to do, we should accomplish nothing; if because Nature's laws are large and comprehensive, we never acted except on the largest principles, we should either fall a prey to unsound generalisations, the more ruinous because of their grandeur, or we should become paralysed with a Turkish fatalism. Far better, no doubt, to make the utmost use of what precise knowledge we have,

however little may be the amount of it, and not to suffer
our minds to be bewildered by coping too freely with an
adversary whose play is beyond us.   It is these humble,
cautiously inductive people that prosper most in the world
up to a certain point.   To them belong the large populations, the thriving communities, the stable politics.   They
never dream of defying Nature; they win an endless series
of small victories over her.

There is no reason why this cautiousness should necessarily degenerate into little-mindedness.   It does not take its
beginning in any deficiency of the feeling for what is great.
On the contrary, it is the direct result of an overwhelming
sense of the greatness and, so to speak, the dangerousness
of Nature.   Those who proceed thus warily, probing Nature
as they go, may with most reason expect to penetrate far
and to elevate their minds gradually until they can venture
to cope with the grandeur of the world and become familiar
with great ideas.   And when this is done they will have
escaped the danger of atheism.   Their minds will become
the mirror of an Infinite Being, and their whole natures will
be conformed to His.   But in the earlier stages of such a
process the temptation to a kind of atheism is strong.   From
the habit of leaving out of account all larger considerations
in every problem, on the ground that they are vague and
not precisely calculable, they are led easily to forget the very
existence of such considerations.   The habit of never suffering the mind to dwell on anything great produces often an
atheism of the most pitiable and helpless kind.   The soul
of man lives upon the contemplation of laws or principles;
it is made to be constantly assimilating such sustenance from

the Universe; this is its food; *not by bread only, but by every word that proceedeth out of the mouth of God doth man live.* What then must be the moral starvation of the man who, from an excess of caution, turns away from everything of the kind, until from want of habit he can no longer see such things, and forgets their very existence; so that for him there is no longer any glory in the Universe?   For all beauty or glory is but the presence of law; and the Universe to him has ceased to be a scene of law and has become an infinite litter of detail, a rubbish-heap of confused particulars, a mere worry and weariness to the imagination.   I have been describing the Philistine, the abject slave of details, who worships a humiliated, dissected, and abject deity, a mere Dagon, "fallen flat upon the grundsel-edge, and shaming his worshippers."

There is a particular extreme form of conventionalism which all men who observe it instinctively call by the name of atheism.   Who has not said to himself, in reading the history of the French Revolution, that possibly the most genuine atheist where so many professed atheism may have been among the orthodox defenders of the old régime?   Of the Revolutionists we are disposed to say that surely they must have had some kind of belief, else whence came their energy? but among the crowd of Voltairian Abbés we can fancy some in whom the conflict between inherited and imbibed ways of thinking may have destroyed belief and energy alike.   Those who live in the decay of Churches and systems of life are exposed to such a paralysis.   They have been made all that they are by the system; their mode of thought and feeling, their very morality, has grown out of it.   But at

a given moment the system is struck with decay. It falls
out of the current of life and thought. Then the faith
which had long been genuine, even if mistaken, which had
actually inspired vigorous action and eloquent speech, begins
to ebb. The vigour begins to be spasmodic, the eloquence
to ring hollow, the loyalty to have an air of hopeless self-
sacrifice. Faith gradually passes into conventionalism. A
later stage comes when the depression, the uneasiness, the
misgivings, have augmented tenfold. It is then that in an
individual here and there the moral paralysis sets in. In
the ardour of conflict they have pushed into the foreground
all the weakest parts of their creed, and have learnt the
habit of asserting most vehemently just what they doubt
most, because it is what is most denied. As their own belief
ebbs away from them they are precluded from learning a
new one, because they are too deeply pledged, have promised too much, asseverated too much, and involved too
many others with themselves. Happy those in such a situation who either are not too clear-sighted or cling to a system
not entirely corrupt! There is an extreme case when what
is upheld as divine has really become a source of moral
evil, while the champion is one who cannot help seeing
clearly. As he becomes reluctantly enlightened, as his
advocacy grows first a little forced, then by degrees consciously hypocritical, until in the end he secretly confesses
himself to be on the wrong side,—what a moral dissolution!
Henceforth he sees in the Universe nothing but a chaos.
The law which once he fancied he discerned there, he can
recognise no longer, and yet is forbidden by his situation
from recognising any other. The link that bound him to

the Universe is snapped ; the motive that inspired his actions
is gone, and his actions have become meaningless, mechanical, galvanic.  He is an Atheist, without a God because
without a law.  Such men may often be noted among the
most intelligent adherents of expiring causes, demoralised
soldiers, powerless for good, though sometimes capable of
mischief.

These are specimens of what seems to be properly
atheism.  The common characteristic of all such states of
mind is feebleness.  In the first example you have violent
feebleness, impotence ; in the second, cautious feebleness ;
in the third, cynical feebleness ; but in all cases feebleness
springing from a conscious want of any clue to the order of
the Universe.  These specimens are all such as may be
furnished by men of great natural vigour.  The cynical
atheist has often an extreme subtlety of intellect, the
Philistine commonly begins with a great grasp of reality, a
great superiority to illusions ; the wilful atheist has often
much imagination and energy.  Where a character wanting
in energy is infected by atheism you have those ἀμένηνα
κάρηνα of which the world is at all times full.  By the side
of the profound cynic you have the mere lounger, who can
take an interest in nothing, all whose thoughts are hearsays,
never verified, never realised, not believed, not worthy of
the name of prejudices—echoes of prejudices, imitations of
hypocrisy.  He moves about embarrassed and paralysed by
the hollowness of all he knows ; conscious that nothing that
he has in his mind would bear the smallest criticism or probation, knowing no way to anything better, and meanwhile
ingenuously confessing his own inanity.  By the side of the

over-judicious Philistine, who has fallen into feebleness through an excessive dread of generalising hastily, there may be seen the born Philistine, who does not know, and has never heard, what generalising is, who becomes uncomfortable when he hears a principle enunciated, as if he had been addressed by a foreigner in some language unknown to him, and whose homely talk never willingly travels beyond what time the train starts, and whether it happened on Monday or on Tuesday.   Lastly, by the side of the brilliant Utopian, who overlooks the greatness of the Necessity with which he has to contend, there is the Utopian without brilliancy, the *enragé*, the mere restless disturber.

As Atheism is but another name for feebleness, so the universal characteristic of Theology—if we put aside for the present the belief, rare till lately, in an utterly hostile or thwarting Deity—is energy.   He who has a faith, we know well, is twice himself.   The world, the conventional or temporary order of things, goes down before the weapons of faith, before the energy of those who have a glimpse, or only think they have a glimpse, of the eternal or normal order of things.   And this vigour of Theism does not much depend on the nature of the God in whom the theist believes.   Just as Atheism does not consist in a bad theory of the Universe, but in the want of any theory, so Theism consists not in possessing a meritorious or true or consoling theory, but simply in possessing a theory of the Universe. He who has such a theory acts with confidence and decision, he who has no such theory is paralysed.   One of the rudest of all theories of the Universe is that propounded by Mohammed, yet it raised up a dispersed nation to vigour,

union, and empire.   Calvinism presents assuredly a view of
the Universe which is not in any way consoling, yet this
creed too has given vigour and heroism.   The creed of the
earliest Romans rested upon no basis which could for a
moment pass for philosophical, yet while it was believed it
gave order to the state, sanction to morality, victory to the
armies.   Whatever kind of Theology be in question, so long
as it is truly believed, the only danger is of its inspiring too
much energy, of its absorbing its votaries too much, and
driving them into extreme courses.

And so if the Nature recognised by Science be not
benevolent, and have provided no future life for men, it
does not follow that her votaries are not theologians, and it
is quite clear that their theology gives them energy.   Many
theologies have admitted no future life—indeed our own, in
its earlier Judaic form, laid no stress upon any future life.
And it is not the benevolence of his Deity which gives so
much energy and confidence to the convinced theist; it is
rather the assurance that he has the secret of propitiating
his Deity.   It was not because Jupiter or Mars were benevolent beings that the Roman went out to battle confiding
in their protection.   It was because all sacrifices had been
performed which the Pontiffs or the Sibylline Books pre-
scribed.   Just of the same kind is the theistic vigour which
we see in modern Science.   Science also has its *procuratio
prodigiorum.*   It does not believe that Nature is benevolent,
and yet it has all the confidence of Mohammedans or
Crusaders.   This is because it believes that it understands
the laws of Nature, and that it knows how to deal so that
Nature shall favour its operations.   Not by the Sibylline

Books, but by experiment, not by supplications but by
scientific precautions and operations it discovers and pro-
pitiates the mind of its Deity.

The advance of Science then is by no means equivalent
to the advance of Atheism.   But what shall we say of that
other advancing Power which terrifies religious men, and
which calls itself the Revolution?   The Revolution in
Europe delights in declaring itself atheistic.   So far as it is
really so, by being Titanic, it is doomed to failure.   But
beyond this its invectives against God and against religion
do not prove that it is atheistic, but only that it thinks itself
so.   And why does it think itself so?   Because God and
religion are identified in its view with the Catholic Church,
and the Catholic Church is a thing so very redoubtable
that we need scarcely inquire why it is passionately hated
and feared.   But then the Catholic Church is *not* really
identical with theism, or even with Christianity.   We cannot
expect an angry party to draw these distinctions, but they
are so plain that there remains nothing to discuss.   There
is plenty in the Catholic Church of what is oppressive and
repugnant to the modern spirit, even if we make abstraction
of all its Christianity.   And when we hear the charges
which the Revolution brings against it, such as affinity with
despotism, with aristocratic privilege, with sacerdotalism or
with militarism, we see plainly that it is not hated even for
its Christianity, much less for its theism.   Christianity in its
original character had an evident analogy with that modern
liberal movement which assails Catholicism.   It breathed
something of the spirit of equality, and still more of the
spirit of fraternity; it took its rise in a bold rebellion

against sacerdotal authority.  But even if this were otherwise, it would remain true that the Revolution assails not
theology itself but only a particular theology embodied in a
particular institution.  For another theology is quite conceivable which so far from thwarting the Revolution might
embody all its aspirations.

Equality, brotherhood between classes and nations,—are
these ideas so radically inconsistent with theology that they
cannot be realised until theology has been swept away?  So
far from it that if we did not know historically by what
process Catholic theology became allied with caste and
privilege so far as to compromise itself, we should have
thought such an unnatural alliance scarcely possible.  In
France theology was found on the side of privilege, but in
the Moslem East the equality of mankind has been preached,
and successfully, in the name of theology.  If a Christian
preacher had been inspired to do so, he might with perfect
warrant from his religion have proclaimed Equality in
France.  Indeed this was to some extent what actually
happened.  Rousseau spoke partly in the name of theology,
and even of Christian theology; one school among the
revolutionists was fond of remarking the analogy between
the revolutionary doctrine and early Christianity; and it
was not until the sceptical foundation had been in a manner
abandoned, and an appeal made to religion, that the spirit
of political change awoke.

But the Revolution has also, no doubt, a quarrel with
theology as a doctrine.  "Theology," it says, "even if not
exactly opposed to social improvement, is a superstition, and
as such allied to ignorance and conservatism.  Granting

that its precepts are good, it enforces them by legends and fictitious stories which can only influence the uneducated, and therefore in order to preserve its influence it must needs oppose education. Nor are these stories a mere excrescence of theology, but theology itself. For theology is neither more nor less than a doctrine of the supernatural. It proclaims a power behind nature which occasionally interferes with natural laws. It proclaims another world quite different from this in which we live, a world into which what is called the soul is believed to pass at death. It believes, in short, in a number of things which students of nature know nothing about and which science puts aside either with respect or with contempt. These supernatural doctrines are not merely a part of theology, still less separable from theology, but theology consists exclusively of them. Take away the supernatural Person, miracles, and the spiritual world, you take away theology at the same time, and nothing is left but simple Nature and simple Science." Thus theology comes to be used in the sense of supernaturalism, and in this view also excites the hostility of the age. Not merely scientific men themselves, for of these I am not now speaking, but Liberals in general, all those who have any tincture of science, all whose minds have in any degree taken the scientific stamp, a vast number already, and, as education spreads, likely to become coextensive with civilised mankind, form a habit of thought with which they are led to consider theology irreconcilable.

It is a singular coincidence which has combined in apparent opposition to theology the two mightiest forces of the present age, that is, the Revolution and Science. But it is only a coincidence, though ready theorists will never be content to see nothing more in it. They will not admit that theology has been undeservedly charged with all the sins of that ancient corporation called the Catholic Church, with which sins in reality it had nothing whatever to do. It is much more interesting to imagine the Church as the body of which theology is the soul, and to trace all the body's actions to the natural disposition of the informing soul. By this easy process we arrive at the conclusion that theology is an essentially conservative and stagnant principle, with the strongest natural affinity for despotism, privilege, respectability, and every kind of antiquated pretension, that, in short, it is a way of viewing the Universe which inevitably leads to all the vices peculiar to old endowed corporations. And that an institution which is opposed to the Revolution should be at the same time at war with Science will never be thought a mere coincidence. Party-spirit will be adroit enough to make it out that Science and Revolution are as soul and body on the one side, as theology and conservatism are on the other; that people who believe in miracles must necessarily side with capital against labour, and that large standing armies follow logically from a belief in benevolent design.

As to the mistake which lies in confounding theology with supernaturalism it is not necessary here to do more than repeat shortly what was said in the first chapter. First, then, there is no necessary connection between theology and supernaturalism. It is quite possible to believe in a God, and even a personal God, of whom Nature is the complete and only manifestation. Supernaturalism is part of the reigning theology, but it is not any necessary part of theology, as such.   Secondly, when supernaturalism is said to be *identical* with theology, this is not true at all, even of the reigning theology.   It is simply a mistake which has arisen from taking literally an abbreviated form of expression by which in controversy the controversialist is identified with the thesis he happens to be maintaining for the moment. He is said to fall when his thesis falls, though in reality he may remain as prosperous as ever.   Thus Catholicism is identified in controversy with certain doctrines which Protestantism disputes, transubstantiation, worship of the Virgin, etc., and yet if these doctrines were to fall it is quite conceivable that the Catholic Church, so far from falling, might flourish more than ever.   In the same way, in controversy with science the reigning theology and supernaturalism are convertible terms.   That is to say, if supernaturalism is refuted, science wins and the reigning theology loses in the particular controversy in which they are engaged.   In the controversial sense this is the destruction of theology, but only in the controversial sense.   For when the worship of God outside Nature is taken away the worship of God in Nature remains.   Whether this residue is important or unimportant will be considered later ; at any rate it is there ; and it would not be surprising if it should turn out more considerable than controversialists believe, when we remember how habitual it is for controversialists to exaggerate their differences.

At any rate, it is evident that the theology of the book of Job, of many of the Psalms, *e.g.* the 104th, of many passages in the Prophets, of many discourses of Christ, of many passages in the Epistles, would remain unaffected if Supernaturalism were entirely abandoned.   No more need be said at this stage.

I conclude then that the prevalent opinion about the advance of atheism rests upon an abuse of the word "atheism."   The threatening alliance between Science and the Revolution is not really directed in favour of atheism nor against theology.   For the antagonist of Science is only supernaturalism and not theology as such, while Science itself has all the character of a theology, such as theologies were at the first, being capable of inspiring a fanatical zeal and bearing in its hand a budget of practical reforms ; and moreover the Deity it proclaims is not different from the Deity of Christians, but only a too much disregarded aspect of Him.   As to the Revolution, its antagonist is not theology at all, nor even supernaturalism, except in a secondary degree.   The Revolution is infuriated against an ancient corporation, the greatest by far of all corporate bodies ever known, on the ground that in addition to its formidable power it has something antiquated in its constitution, shelters many abuses, and has in the latest centuries made common cause with other declining institutions.   This corporation happens to be the depositary of a theology partly supernaturalistic, but we can see plainly that had it been the depositary of modern science itself it would have excited just the same animosity, nay, probably very much more, for in fact its creed in some aspects is in most remarkable agreement with the revolutionary creed itself.

On the other hand, of atheism, that demoralising palsy of human nature, which consists in the inability to discern in the Universe any law by which human life may be guided, there is in the present age less danger than ever, and it is daily made more and more impossible by science itself: of revolt against the Christian law of Fraternity, there is also less than ever in this age, and that redemption of the poor and that pacification of nations which Christianity first suggested are more prominent than ever among the aspirations of mankind.  At the same time the organisation of the Church seems ill adapted to the age, and seems to expose it to the greatest danger; and, what is far more serious, the old elevating communion with God, which Christianity introduced, seems threatened by the new scientific theology, which, while presenting to us deeper views than ever of His infinite and awful greatness, and more fascinating views than ever of His eternal beauty and glory, denies for the present to Him that human tenderness, justice and benevolence which Christ taught us to see in Him.

# CHAPTER III

INSTEAD of Atheism then, we find that the result of cancelling supernaturalism and submitting to Science is a theology in which all men, whether they consider it or not, do actually agree—that which is concerned with God in Nature.  I do not here raise the question of causes or laws ; let it be allowed that Nature is merely the collective name of a number of coexistences and sequences, and that God is merely a synonym for Nature.  Let all this be allowed, or let the contrary of this be allowed.  Such controversies may be raised about the human as well as about the Divine Being.  Some may consider the human body as the habitation of a soul distinct and separable from it ; others may refuse to recognise any such distinction : some may maintain that man is merely the collective name for a number of processes : some may consider the human being as possessing a free will and as being independent of circumstances ; others may regard him as the necessary product of a long series of physical influences.  All these differences may be almost as important as they seem to the disputants who are occupied about them, but after all they do not affect the fact that the human being is there, and they do not prevent us from regarding him with strong feelings. The same is true of the Divine Being. Whatever may be questioned, it is certain that we are in the presence of an Infinite and Eternal Being; except through some of those perversions which I described in the last chapter, we cannot help the awe and admiration with which we contemplate Him; we cannot help recognising that our wellbeing depends on taking a right view of His nature.

But if theology in a certain sense of the word would survive the disappearance of supernaturalism, how would it be with religion? Are we to regard religion as identical with theology, or are we to suppose that the popular instinct, which is keenly alive to all that affects religion, but at the same time pretty indifferent to the fate of theology, is right in drawing so broad a distinction between them?

There are two ways in which the mind apprehends any object, two sorts of knowledge which combine to make complete and satisfactory knowledge. The one may be called theoretic or scientific knowledge; the other practical, familiar, or imaginative knowledge. The greatest trial of human nature lies in the difficulty of reconciling these two kinds of knowledge, of preventing them from interfering with one another, of arranging satisfactory relations between them. In order of time the second kind of knowledge has the precedence, and avails itself of this advantage to delay and impede the arrival of the first kind. Before the stars, the winds, the trees and plants could be grasped scientifically and the laws which govern them ascertained, they had been grasped, and as it were appropriated, by the human mind experimentally and imaginatively. The latter kind of knowledge was in some respects better than the former. It was more intimate and realised, so that, as far as it was true, it was more available. For practical purposes, accurate scientific knowledge of a thing is seldom sufficient. To obtain complete practical command over it you must take possession of it with the imagination and feelings as well as the reason, and it will often happen that this imaginative knowledge, helped very slightly by scientific knowledge, carries a man practically further than a very perfect scientific knowledge by itself. Witness the instinctive, as we say, and unanalysable skill sometimes possessed by savages. Moreover, this kind of knowledge is more attractive and interesting, and so has a more powerful modifying influence upon its possessor than the other kind, for the simple reason that it takes hold of the most plastic side of his nature. But just because it is so fascinating, and is at the same time not by itself trustworthy, it has certain mischievous consequences when it comes, as it generally does, first. Then it fills the mind with prejudices, hasty misconceptions, which, seizing upon the imagination, are stereotyped in the form of superstitions ; and these sometimes exercise by themselves a most pernicious influence, and in any case close the mind against the entrance of the sounder scientific knowledge. When this imaginative medley of observation and prejudice has long had possession, Science arrives. There follows a contest between the two kinds of knowledge, in which the human being suffers much. Truth cannot in the long run be resisted, and so, after whatever defence, the fortress is carried and the phantom garrison of superstition is driven

out.   The mind passes now under a new set of impressions,
and places itself in a new relation to the Universe.   Its
victory over superstition has been won by placing a careful
restraint upon imagination and feeling.   In order not to be
misled by feeling, it has been forced artificially to deaden
feeling; lest the judgment should be overwhelmed by the
impressiveness of the Universe, it arms itself with callousness;
it turns away from Nature the sensitive side, and receives
the shock upon the adamantine shield of the sceptical
reason.   In this way it substitutes one imperfect kind ot
knowledge for another.   Before, it realised strongly, but
scarcely analysed at all; now, it analyses most carefully, but
ceases in return to realise.   As the victory of the scientific
spirit becomes more and more decided, there passes a deep
shudder of discomfort through the whole world of those
whose business is with realising, and not with testing knowledge.   Religion is struck first, because the whole work of
realising presupposes faith, and yet, as the testing process
comes late, faith is almost always more or less premature.
But poetry and art suffer in their turn.   How full has
modern poetry been of this complaint!   One poet laments
that "Science withdraws the veil of enchantment from
Nature"; one exclaims that "there *was* an awful rainbow
*once* in heaven," but that Science has destroyed it; another
declares that "we murder to dissect," that we should not be
always seeking, but use "a wise passiveness" in the presence
of Nature; another "that Nature made undivine is now
seen slavishly obeying the law of gravitation"; another buries
himself in past ages "when men could still hear from God
heavenly truth in earthly speech, and did not rack their brains."

And yet to complain of the march of the scientific spirit seems as idle as to complain of the law of gravitation itself. It cannot be prevented, even if we were able to show that it ought to be prevented; it cannot much be retarded, even though some danger might be saved by putting the drag upon the wheels of discovery. The ardour of investigation, the fanaticism of truth-worship, make men deaf to such prudential considerations, and they are seconded by all the ill-will that the reigning system has provoked during its long predominance and by all the eager ambitions which the prospect of a revolutionary change awakens. But we may look forward to a time when this transition shall be over, and when a new reconciliation shall have taken place between the two sorts of knowledge. In that happier age true knowledge, scientific, not artificially humanised, will reign without opposition, but the claims of Science once for all allowed, the mind will also apprehend the Universe imaginatively, realising what it knows.

That kind of imaginative eclipse which an object suffers when the shadow of science passes over it has obscured in turn the material universe and Man and God. Natural mythology has become almost incomprehensible to us. The "fair humanities of old religion," which found objects of love in trees and streams, and covered the celestial map with fantastic living shapes—all this has long ago disappeared. More recently Man has been subjected to the analysing process. The mechanical laws which were traced in the physical world, it was long hoped, would never suffice to explain the human being; he at least would remain always mysterious, spiritual, sacred. But now Man begins to reckon

his own being among things more than half explained;
nerve-force, he thinks, is a sort of electricity; man differs
greatly indeed, but not generically, from the brutes. All
this has, for the time at least, the effect of desecrating
human nature.  To the imagination human nature becomes
a thing blurred and spoiled, not really because the new view
of it is in itself degrading, but because the imagination had
realised it otherwise, and cannot in any short time either
part with the old realising or perfect a new one.  Lastly,
science turns her smoked eye-glass upon God, deliberately
diminishing the glory of what she looks at that she may distinguish better.  Here too she sees mechanism where will,
purpose, and love had been supposed before; she drops the
name God, and takes up the less awful name of Nature
instead.

This disenchantment more than any other has made us
ask ourselves whether analysis is not a kind of sacrilege, and
perhaps not merely because in this instance it strikes the
highest object, but for another reason.  Science cannot
easily destroy our feeling for human beings.  We are in such
close contact with our own kind, our imagination and affections take such fast hold of our fellow-men, as to defy physiology.  If it were otherwise we should want a word—
*Ananthropism*—to answer to Atheism.  The thing is indeed
sometimes to be seen, and alarm has lately been expressed
in Germany at the havoc which devotion, probably too exclusive and ambitious, to physical science may make with
the feelings.  But hitherto the scientific disbelief in Humanity
—for so it may be called—has been rare.  As for the material
universe, that indeed has long been almost completely dese-

crated, so that sympathy, communion with the forms of
Nature, is pretty well confined to poets, and is generally
supposed to be an amiable madness in them. But this evil
had another origin. Not analysis but rather religion itself,
and especially monasticism, is responsible for it. In the
ages called "of faith" it was felt even more painfully than
now, so that Chaucer complains of the preachings and ban-
nings of "limitours and other holy frères," which according
to him had banished the fairies from the land. Nature had
been made not merely a dead thing, but a disgusting and
hideous thing, by superstitions of imps, witches, and demons;
so much so that Goethe celebrates science as having actually
restored Nature to the imagination and driven away the
Walpurgis-nacht of the middle ages; and, indeed, by turning attention upon the natural world, and inducing many to
become familiar with its beauties, Science may have given
back to the imagination, in this department, as much as it
has taken away.

But the conception of God is so vast and elevated that
the human mind easily sinks altogether below it. The task
of realising what is too great to be realised, of reaching with
the imagination and growing with the affections to a reality
almost too high for the one, and almost too awful for the
other, is in itself exceptionally difficult. To do this, and yet
at the same time carefully to restrain the imagination and
feelings as Science prescribes, is almost impossible; yet those
who perpetually study Nature, if they study in a healthy and
natural manner, will always in some sense feel the presence
of God. The unity of what they study will sometimes come
home to them and give a sense of awe and delight, if not of

E

love.  But upon those who do not study Nature the advance
of Science and the rumour of its discoveries can have no
other effect than to root out of their minds the very conception of God.  The negative effect is not counterbalanced
by any positive one.  To their apprehensions, if the supernatural Person whose will holds the Universe together is
taken away, the Universe falls at once to pieces.  No other
unity takes His place, and out of the human mind there
perishes the most elevating thought, and out of human life
the chief and principal sacredness.  The remedy for this is
to be found in the study of Nature becoming universal.
Let all be made acquainted with natural laws ; let all form
the habit of contemplating them, and atheism in its full
sense will become a thing impossible, when no mind shall
be altogether without the sense, at once inspiring and sober-
ing, of an eternal order.

But these remarks on the difficulty of harmonising the
scientific with the imaginative knowledge of things, are by
way of digression.  Our business at present is with the fact
that knowledge is of these two kinds, and that the complete
or satisfactory knowledge of anything comes from combining
them.  When the object of knowledge is God, the first kind
of knowledge is called theology, and the second may be
called religion.  By theology the nature of God is ascertained
and false views of it eradicated from the understanding ; by
religion the truths thus obtained are turned over in the mind
and assimilated by the imagination and the feelings.

When it is said, as we hear it said so commonly now,
that the knowledge of God is impossible to man, and therefore that theology is no true science, of course the word

God is used in that peculiar sense of which I have spoken above. Nature every one admits that we know or may know; but of any occult cause of phenomena, or of any supernatural being accomplishing his purpose through natural laws or suspending the course of them, it is denied that we can know anything. Nevertheless since every sort of theology agrees that the laws of Nature are the laws of God, it is evident that in knowing Nature we do precisely to the same extent know God. Regarded in this way, we may say of God that so far from being beyond knowledge, He is the one object of knowledge, and that everything we can know, every proposition we can frame, relates to Him.

It has long been customary, especially with the religious party, to put aside this distinction as perfectly idle. " It is pantheism," they cry, " and pantheism is practically not distinguishable from atheism. A distinction merely speculative has no concern with the most momentous of all practical controversies. Was it not the old maxim of theology that the knowledge of God was life and the ignorance of Him darkness and death? Try and adapt this maxim to your Universe-God. It either loses its meaning altogether, or sinks into some frigid platitude to the effect that all knowledge is valuable, or that the more things you know the more dangers you will be in a condition to avoid."

But here we are reminded of that coincidence between the language of theology and the language lately adopted by science which was our starting-point. Scientific men *do* now tell us in the very language of theology that all hope, that all happiness lies in the knowledge of Nature, and by Nature they mean the Universe. Spontaneously, and in the very act of opposing theology they create theology anew. For they show us that it is not necessary to look beyond Nature or. beyond experience in order to find that unique Object of which theology speaks. They themselves have found Him in Nature itself, where the religious party tell us it is vain to look for Him. The conception of Nature or of the Universe has now acquired distinctness, so that the study of it may be compared with other studies and recommended as specially important.

But how can the conception of the Universe have distinctness, since the Universe includes everything? How can the study of it be compared with other studies?

"What is there, then, that can possibly be studied besides the Universe?"

There is in the first place a would-be reflexion of the Universe, which it is possible to study as if it were the Universe itself; that is, the multitude of traditional unscientific opinions about the Universe. In one sense, these opinions are part of the Universe, and to study them from the historic point of view is to study the Universe; but when they are accepted and studied as a trustworthy counterpart, as they are by all the votaries of authority or tradition, then they may be regarded as a spurious Universe outside the real one, and such students of opinion may be said to study, and yet not to study the Universe.

This spurious Universe is almost as great as the genuine one. There are many profoundly learned men whose thoughts are solely occupied with it and have no concern whatever with reality. The simplest peasant who from living much in the open air has found for himself, unconsciously, some rules to guide him in divining the weather, knows something about the real Universe; but an indefatigable student who has stored a prodigious memory with what the schoolmen have thought, what the philosophers have thought, what the Fathers have thought, may yet have no real knowledge; he may have been busy only with the reflected Universe. Not that the thoughts of dead thinkers stored up in books are not part of the Universe as much as wind and rain; not that they may not repay study quite as well; they are deposits of the human mind, and by studying them much may be discovered about the human mind, the ways of its operation, the stages of its development. As a reflexion too, imperfect yet not wholly unfaithful, of the Universe they may tell much about it. But they become a spurious Universe, and the knowledge of them becomes a false knowledge, when they are studied for themselves only or are confounded with the true Universe. Those who confound commentatorship with philosophy and mistake erudition for science, may be said to study, but not to study the Universe.

There are other classes of men of whom much the same may be said. The scientific school, when they recommend the study of Nature, do not mean, for example, the mere collecting of facts however authentic. Nature with them is not a heap of phenomena, but laws discerned in phenomena, and by a knowledge of Nature they mean a just conception of laws much more than an ample store of information about phenomena. Again, in an age like the present, when methods of inquiry have been laid down and tested by large experience, they do not dignify with the name of the study

of Nature any investigation, however earnest or fresh, of
the facts of the world, which does not conform to these
methods, or show reason for not doing so.

Knowledge of Nature understood in this sense, and
obtained in this manner, is now recommended as the only
true wisdom.    And assuredly it deserves to be called in the
strictest sense Theology.    If God be the Ruler of the
world, as the orthodox theology teaches, the laws of Nature
are the laws by which He rules it.    If you prefer the Pantheistic view, they are the very manifestations of the Divine
Nature.    In any case the knowledge of Nature, if only it
be properly sifted from the corrupting mixture of mere
opinion, is the knowledge of God.    That there may be
another and deeper knowledge of God beyond it does not
affect this fact.

All this is said in answer to the religious party which
denies that there is any practical difference between
pantheism (for so they call the doctrine of a God revealed
in Nature) and atheism.    It is an answer which may seem
to treat theology as a mere synonym for science.

But we may distinguish a particular aspect of science
which more than other aspects deserves to be called theological.

Considered in its practical bearings upon human life, the
study of Nature resolves itself into the study of two things,
a force within the human being, and a necessity without
him.    Life, in short, is like a mechanical problem, in which
a power is required to be so advantageously applied as to
overcome a weight which is greater than itself.    The power
is the human will, the weight is Nature, the motive of the

struggle between them is certain ideals which man instinctively puts before himself—an ideal of happiness, or an ideal
of perfection.  By means of Science he is enabled to apply
the power in the most advantageous manner.  Every piece
of knowledge he acquires helps him in his undertaking.
Every special science which he perfects removes a new set
of obstacles, procures him a new set of resources.  And in
his conflict with natural difficulties his energy and hope are
in proportion to his power of measuring the force he has,
and the resistance he will meet with.  When he is able to
measure this precisely, his hope becomes confidence, even
in circumstances which might seem the most alarming.
We allow ourselves to be hurried through the air at the rate
of fifty miles an hour, with a noise and impetus appalling to
a bystander, and all the while read or sleep comfortably.
Why?  Because the forces we have set in motion are all
accurately measured, the obstacles to be met fully known.
When the measurement is only approximate, there is not
confidence, but only hope predominating over fear.  The
experienced sailor feels this; he trusts himself to the perils
of the sea, because he knows that he is pretty well matched
against the necessity he provokes, though he cannot know
that he is the superior, because he can calculate a good
many of the dangers, though not all.

Thus it is in each of the separate undertakings that make
up life.  To each of them belongs its appropriate knowledge,
upon which our equanimity and repose of mind, as far as
the particular undertaking is concerned, depend.  But life
itself, taken as a whole, is an undertaking.  Life itself has
its objects which make it interesting to us, which lead us to

bear the burden of it.    These objects, like those minor ones,
are only to be attained by a struggle between the power Will
and the weight Nature, and in this struggle also both success and the hope of success depend upon a certain knowledge which may enable us to apply the power with advantage.    But the knowledge required in this case is of a more
general kind; it is not a knowledge confined to certain sets
of phenomena, and giving us a power correspondingly
limited, but it is a general knowledge of the relation in
which human life stands to the Universe, and of the means
by which life may be brought into the most satisfactory
adaptation to it.    Now, by what name shall we call this
knowledge?

Every one has his general views of human life, which are
more or less distinct.    Upon these general views more than
upon anything else connected with the understanding moral
character depends.    For though theoretically morality may
be independent of all such views, practically and in the long
run it varies with them.    "What has life to give?    How far
does it lend itself to our ideals?"    These questions lie outside moral philosophy, and yet they are as vital to morality
as any that lie within it.    They are also quite as important
to human happiness as all particular measures contrived to
increase human happiness.    No man fights with any heart
if he thinks he has Nature against him.    He who believes
that men are not made to be happy, will lose the energy to
do even what can be done for their happiness; he who
meets with more than a certain degree of discouragement in
the pursuit of virtue, will give it up.

Of an unfavourable view of human life there are three

principal consequences—crime, languor, and suicide. The majority of crimes, and still more of meannesses, perhaps, are not committed from bad intentions, but from a despair of human life. "I am sorry, but I *must* do it; I am driven to it; everybody has to do it; we must look at things as they are;" these are the reflections which lead men into violations of morality. The feeling that life will not always allow us to do what is right, faint perhaps in each individual mind, grows strong when many who share it come together; it grows stronger by being uttered, stronger still by being acted upon; it creates an atmosphere of laxity; morality retires more and more out of view; until the thought of crime itself, and even of enormous crime, becomes familiar, and at last is carried almost unconsciously into act. It is not, then, from want of morality that men do wrong, but from want of another sort of knowledge. They know what is right and what is wrong; it is not from overlooking this distinction that they fall into the wrong, nor would they escape the danger by reflecting upon it ever so much. What determines their action is a belief in some sort of necessity, some fatality with which it is vain to struggle; it is a general view of human life as unfavourable to ideals.

Another such general view of human life produces apathy. A man who has persuaded himself that we are the creatures of circumstance, or that we are the victims of a necessity with which it is impossible for us to cope, will give up the battle with Nature and do nothing. Perhaps he has his head full of instances of the best endeavours after improvement failing entirely, or by some fatality producing extreme unhappiness; of the purest and noblest labours causing

mischief which complete inactivity would have avoided;
how Queen Isabella introduced the Inquisition; how Las
Casas initiated the slave-trade; how pauperism has been over
and over again fostered by philanthropy; how the Prince of
Peace Himself, according to His own saying, brought a sword
upon the earth.    He may think that human life, as it runs
on naturally, is not a bad thing, but that all attempts to control it or improve it are hopeless; that all high ideals are
merely ambitious; that purpose and, still more, system and
all sophistication of life are mischievous.    And so he may
come to renounce all free-will, he may yield to the current
of ordinary affairs, and become a mere conventionalist,
accommodating himself to whatever he does not like, and
learning gradually to tolerate with complete indifference the
most enormous evils.    Against such a perversion of mind
morality is no defence; what is needed is not a new view
of what ought to be—such a man knows well enough what
ought to be—but a new view of what can or may be, a more
encouraging view of the Universe.

Sometimes the despair of human life goes to a much
greater length.    Life is a game at which we are not forced
to play; we may at any time throw up the cards.    That
only a few do so proves that more or less consciously most
of us have a general view of life not altogether unfavourable.
We are for the most part hardly aware of this general view,
because it is always the same.    We should become painfully
aware of it if it were suddenly to change.    There is, as it
were, a suicide-mark below which our philosophy is always
liable to sink.    If we came to think life irreconcilably
opposed to our ideals, and at the same time were enthusias-

tically devoted to them, life would become intolerable to us. If our sense of the misery or emptiness of life became for some reason much more keen than it is, life would at last become intolerable to us. Individuals are constantly travelling by both roads to this goal, and there is no reason why whole societies or nations should not in like manner cease to think life valuable. Something of the kind happened with the Stoics of the imperial period. Their philosophy was only just above suicide-mark, and was continually dropping below it. In Asia the same is true of whole popu-‌lations, with whom the value of life has sunk to the very lowest point.

Of all these classes of men we say justly that they want faith. Their criminality or languor or despair are the consequences of their having no faith. But we sometimes express the same thing differently, and say that they have no God, no theology. With our Christian habit of connecting God with goodness and love, we confuse together the notions of a theology and a faith. Let us reflect that it is quite possible to have a theology without having a faith. We may believe in a God, but a God unfavourable, hostile, or indifferent to us. In the same way we may believe in a God neither altogether friendly nor altogether the reverse. Many Pagan theologies were of this kind, and even many Christian sects, while nominally holding the perfect benevol‌ence of God, have practically worshipped a Being who in this respect did not differ from the Pagan deities.

It would be legitimate to call such general views of the relation of Nature to our ideals by the name of theology in all cases, and not merely those particular general views

which are encouraging.  If we believe that Nature helps us
in our strivings, we have both a theology and a faith ; if we
believe that Nature is indifferent to us or hostile to us, we
have no faith, but we have still a theology, for we have still
a definite notion of God's dealings with us.  And this use
of the word is not only justified by its etymology ; it is much
more conformable to actual usage.  To identify theology
with the doctrine of the supernatural is, as I have pointed
out, to narrow the meaning of the word unnaturally, and to
appropriate it to a particular part of a particular theological
system.  A deception is produced by giving this technical
sense to a word which in the common understanding has a
much larger meaning.  When those who reject the supernatural declare theology to be exploded, they are commonly
understood to mean that a vast mass of doctrine, partly
moral, partly historical, partly physical, in which the supernatural is mixed up, is exploded, whereas all they really say
is that just that part is exploded which is supported only by
the evidence of the supernatural.  In like manner it is but
a small part of what is commonly understood by theology
that has to do with final causes, and yet those who consider
final causes not objects of knowledge are fond of drawing
the inference that all theological systems must be systems
of spurious knowledge.  Sometimes this juggle which is
practised with the word theology becomes grotesquely
apparent, and a sceptic will tell us in the same breath that
theology deals with matters entirely beyond the range of
human intellect, and that theology has been refuted by the
discoveries of modern science !

The questions which we all understand to be theological

are such as these : Is there a reward for virtue? Is there a
compensation for undeserved misery? Is there a sure retri-
bution for crime? Is there hope that the vicious man may
become virtuous? Are there means by which the pressure
upon the conscience produced by wrong-doing may be
removed? Are there means by which the mind disposed
to virtue may defend itself from temptation? In one word,
is life worth having, and the Universe a habitable place for
one in whom the sense of duty has been awakened? These
questions are answered in different ways by different men.
But they are answered in some way by all men, even by
those who consider themselves to have no theology at all.
Christianity is the system which answers them in the most
encouraging way. It says that virtue in the long run will
be happy partly in this life, but much more in a life beyond
the grave. It says that misery is partly the punishment of
crime, partly the probation of virtue ; but in the inexhaustible
future which belongs to each individual man there are
equivalents and over-payments for all that part of it which
is undeserved. It says that virtue, when tried, may count
upon help, secret refreshings that come in answer to prayer
—friends providentially sent, perhaps guardian angels. It
says that souls entangled in wrong-doing may raise themselves out of it by a mystic union with Christ, and burdened
consciences be relieved by sharing in the infinite merit of
His self-sacrifice. If you ask on what so happy and inspiring a belief rests, the evidence produced is in part supernatural.

This is not only a theology but a faith, the most triumphant of all faiths. But those who do not heartily share

it or who consciously reject it, yet give *some* answer to these questions.   They have a theology as much as Christians; they must even have a faith of some sort, otherwise they would renounce human life.   It may be stated perhaps much as follows :

"We have not much reason to believe in any future state.   We are content to look at human life as it lies visibly before us.   Surveying it so, we find that it is indeed very different from what we could wish it to be.   It is full of failures and miseries.   Multitudes die without knowing anything that can be called happiness, while almost all know too well what is meant by misery.   The pains that men endure are frightfully intense, their enjoyments for the most part moderate.   They are seldom aware of happiness while it is present, so very delicate a thing is it.   When it is past they recognise for the first time, or perhaps fancy, that it was present.   If we could measure all the happiness there is in the world, we should perhaps be rather pained than gladdened by discovering the amount of it; if we could measure all the misery we should be appalled beyond description.   When from happiness we pass to the moral ideal, again we find the world disappointing.   It is not a sacred place any more than it is a happy place.   Vice and crime very frequently prosper in it.   Some of the worst of men are objects of enthusiastic admiration and emulation.   Some of the best have been hated and persecuted.   Much virtue passes away entirely unacknowledged; much flagrant hypocrisy escapes detection.

"Still on the whole we find life worth having.   The misery we find ourselves able to forget, or callously live through. It is but not thinking, which is always easy, and we become insensible to whatever evil does not affect ourselves. And though the happiness is not great, the variety is. Life is interesting, if not happy. Moreover, in spite of all the injustice of destiny, all the inequality with which fortune is meted out, yet it may be discerned that, at least in the more fortunate societies, justice is the rule and injustice the exception. There are laws by which definite crimes are punished, there is a force of opinion which reaches vaguer offences and visits even the disposition to vice with a certain penalty. Virtue seldom goes without some reward, however inadequate; if it is not recognised generally or publicly, it finds here and there an admirer, it gathers round it a little circle of love; when even this is wanting it often shows a strange power of rewarding itself. On the whole, we are sustained and reconciled to life by a certain feeling of hope, by a belief, resting upon real evidence, that things improve and better themselves around us."

This is certainly a very different faith from Christianity. Whether it deserves to be called a faith at all, whether it justifies men in living and in calling others into life, may be doubted. But it is just as much a theology as Christianity. It deals with just the same questions and gives an answer to them, though a different answer. Both views, whatever may be professed, are views about God. Christianity regards God as a friend; it says that He is Love. The other view regards Him as awful, distant, inhuman, yet not radically hostile.

Of course such views of human life, while they remain thus vague and loose, have nothing scientific about them.

But if they ceased to be vague, if precision were given to
them, we should have a science of the relation of the
Universe to human ideals.    Such a science is constructing
itself fast.    The more men come to know Nature and to
feel confidence in their knowledge, the more eagerly they
will consider what is the attitude of Nature towards human
beings.    This question is not one which is in any way
removed from human knowledge, it is not one which it can
be considered morbid to betray curiosity about.    Yet this
is *the* question of theology.    Not only is it the only question
with which theology ought to be concerned ; it is the only
question with which theology ever has been concerned.
The theologies of the world are merely different attempts to
answer it.    If they have for the most part trespassed upon
the ground of the supernatural, this has not been because
theology is necessarily concerned with the supernatural, but
in some cases because the line between the natural and
supernatural had not been clearly drawn, in some cases
because it was honestly believed that supernatural occurrences had happened and could be authenticated, and that
such occurrences were calculated to throw new light upon
the relation of God to man.    If this belief was a delusion,
theology must learn to confine itself to Nature.    It may
have to alter its idea of God, it may have to regard Him
with fear and cold awe as in the days before the Gospel was
published ; it may even cease to be a faith, and may become
an incubus,—a scientific superstition.    But theology will
remain notwithstanding a perfectly legitimate study, one
which, under that or under some other name, men will
always pursue with an interest they can feel in no other,

one which stands in a more intimate relation than any other
to morality, and must always be taught in conjunction with
morality.

We arrive then at the conclusion that there is a natural
theology which inquires into the relation of the Universe to
human ideals. But here we must beware of a common
misconception. It is often said that when you substitute
Nature for God you take a thing heartless and pitiless
instead of love and goodness. Undoubtedly much less
of love and goodness can be discovered in Nature than
Christians see in God. But when it is said that there are
no such qualities in Nature, that Nature consists of relentless
and ruthless laws, that Nature knows nothing of forgiveness,
and inexorably exacts the utmost penalty for every trans-
gression, a confusion is made between two different meanings which may be given to the word Nature. We are
concerned here with Nature as opposed to that which is
above Nature, not with Nature as opposed to man. We use
it as a name comprehending all the uniform laws of the
Universe as known in our experience, and excluding such
laws as are inferred from experiences so exceptional and
isolated as to be difficult of verification. In this sense
Nature is not heartless or unrelenting; to say so would be
equivalent to saying that pity and forgiveness are in all cases
supernatural. It may be true that the law of gravitation is
quite pitiless, that it will destroy the most innocent and
amiable person with as little hesitation as the wrong-doer.
But there are other laws which are not pitiless. There
are laws under which human beings form themselves into
communities, and set up courts in which the claims of

F

individuals are weighed with careful skill. There are laws
under which churches and philanthropical societies are
formed, under which misery is sought out and relieved and
every evil that can be discovered in the world is redressed.
Nature, in the sense in which we are now using the word,
includes humanity, and therefore, so far from being pitiless,
includes all the pity that belongs to the whole human family,
and all the pity that they have accumulated and, as it were,
capitalised in institutions, political, social, and ecclesiastical,
through countless generations.

If we abandoned our belief in the supernatural it would
not be only inanimate Nature that would be left to us; we
should not give ourselves over, as it is often rhetorically
described, to the mercy of merciless powers—winds and
waves, earthquakes, volcanoes and fire. The God we should
believe in would not be a passionless, utterly inhuman
power. He would indeed be a God often neglecting us in
our need, a God often deaf to prayers. Nature including
Humanity would be our God. We should read His character
not merely in the earthquake and fire, but also in the still
small voice; not merely in the destroying powers of the
world, but, as Mohammed said, in the compassion that we
feel for one another; not merely in the storm that threatens
the sailor with death, but in the lifeboat and the Grace
Darling that put out from shore to the rescue; not merely
in the intricate laws that confound our prudence, but in the
science that penetrates them and the art which makes them
subservient to our purposes; not merely in the social evils
that fill our towns with misery and cover our frontiers with
war, but in the St. Francis that makes himself the brother

of the miserable, and in the Fox and Penn that proclaim principles of peace.

Let us take one of the principal doctrines of the supernatural theology, and observe how it is modified by the rejection of supernaturalism. The eternal happiness reserved for the just is one of these doctrines. No natural evidence can establish it, nor even the future life involved in it. Even when the Psalmist, speaking merely of the present life, wrote, "I have been young, and now am old, and yet saw I never the righteous forsaken, nor his seed begging their bread," he perhaps thought of supernatural interpositions by which evil was averted from the just man. Suppose now that we repudiate all such beliefs, and confine ourselves strictly to the facts of Nature as we discover them from uniform experience. Let us suppose that the ordinary laws of Nature govern the lot of the just man, and that no exemptions are made in his favour. Do we find that these ordinary laws take no account of his justice, and that his prospects are in no respect different from those of the unjust man? Is Nature, as distinguished from the supernatural, regardless of the distinction between virtue and vice? No doubt Nature is not a perfectly just judge. The just man has misfortunes like the unjust; he may suffer from accident or disease. His justice may be denied; he may suffer the penalties of injustice. All this may happen in particular cases, and yet no one doubts that on the whole the just man reaps a reward for his justice. A very simple law operates to reward him. By his justice he benefits the community, and the community, partly out of gratitude, partly out of an interested calculation, repay him for the service he has done. This law fails of its effect in a good number of cases, but in the majority of cases it does not fail. And when it fails, it seldom fails altogether. There is generally some reward for justice, if not always an adequate reward. Accordingly, not only Christians, or those who believe in something more than Nature, but those whose only God is Nature, and even those whose knowledge of Nature is very superficial, fully recognise that virtue is rewarded. "Honesty is the best policy" has become a proverb, and hypocrites have come into existence hoping to secure the reward without deserving it. We see, then, that those who believe in Nature only may be said to believe not only in a God, but, in some sense, in a personal God. Their God, at least, has so much of personality that He takes account of the distinction of virtue and vice, that He punishes crime, and that He relieves distress.

"It is quite true," says Maudsley, writing purely as a physiologist, "that the just man is supported by everlasting arms."

# CHAPTER IV

As theology is to be distinguished from religion, a great dominant system such as Christianity, which is both a theology and a religion, has naturally two distinct classes of opponents. Hitherto I have spoken of those who oppose it as it is a theology, that is, the scientific school, and incidentally I have referred to the Revolution (which sees in Christianity properly neither a theology nor a religion, but a great social and political organisation), in order to show how purely casual is its coalition with Science. It remains to consider the opposition which is made to Christianity as it is a religion.

The scientific school, as such, contents itself with criticism and makes no affirmation in respect of religion. Individual members of it in many cases look forward to nothing but the downfall of religion. Wholly distinct from this school is the party which, while it rejects Christianity, proclaims religion to be the highest of all things and looks forward to a great renewal of its influence. But again we find this party divided within itself as soon as we inquire what the religion is which they regard as destined to replace

Christianity.   One section says that Humanity will be in
future the object of worship, but meanwhile for many
generations past a long line of insinuators have been repeat-
ing under their breath that the time would come when
Pantheism would prevail, when the supernatural tyrant of
the Universe would give way to the Universe itself.   There
are further differences of opinion as to the form which this
Pantheism will take, and often it may be observed that the
purer, sweeter worship which is promised to us is pictured
as a revival of Greek Paganism.

I have tried to show that what is commonly called
Atheism may be less shocking, because less atheistic, than
it seems.   In like manner the new experiments in worship
may be less subversive of the old worship than they seem to
be.   That we ought to worship Man, that St. Paul at Athens
assailed true and not false deities, are propositions which
may after all convey nothing so impious.   The words
religion and worship are commonly and conveniently appropriated to the feelings with which we regard God.   But
those feelings—love, awe, admiration, which together make
up worship—are felt in various combinations for human
beings, and even for inanimate objects.   It is not exclusively
but only *par excellence* that religion is directed towards God.
When feelings of admiration are very strong they find vent in
some act ; when they are strong and at the same time serious
and permanent, they express themselves in recurring acts, and
hence arises ritual, liturgy, and whatever the multitude identifies with religion.   But without ritual, religion may exist in its
elementary state, and this elementary state of religion is what
may be described as *habitual and permanent admiration.*

Now it is surely not to be supposed that every higher form of religion ought to supersede and drive out the lower forms. Difficult no doubt it is to restrain religious feeling from such intolerance. Religious feeling in its exaltation delights to repeat that worship paid to any but the highest object is sin and is apostasy. But this is a way of speaking which involves a somewhat arbitrary restriction upon the meaning of the word worship. Feelings of admiration and devotion are of various degrees, and are excited by various objects. Such feelings may be called by the general name of worship, and we may be said, without offence, to regard an official as worshipful, to worship a wife, to worship heroes. But the same word may also be used in a special and technical sense to denote the particular sort of devotion paid to the highest object we recognise, and it is in this sense alone that the word is used when religion forbids worship to be paid to whatever is in any degree worshipful. Churches however are often intolerant in pushing this way of speaking beyond bounds. The greatest religious revolution in history is, in the main, simply a reaction against such intolerance, when the right of ideal humanity to receive worship was asserted in the heart of a people devoted to the exclusive worship of Deity. And in modern history there are many evidences of a reaction secretly in progress against the absorption of that earlier and lower form of religion which may be called physical by the higher forms. Paganism itself, many think—and why should it not be true?—was too intolerantly put down. Even if the intolerance of a necessary and beneficent revolution is pardonable, that is no reason why it should not be repaired in later and

quieter times. The horror of physical nature which marked
the middle ages has passed away from the modern mind;
the iconoclasm which raged against Greek art and heathen
learning is no more necessary to Christianity than the hatred
of painted windows is to Protestantism. The worship of
natural forms has gradually revived. They now receive a
secondary and inferior sort of homage, and so much in this
respect has the world advanced that there is little danger of
any worship we may pay to natural beauty blunting our
sense of the higher reverence due to moral goodness.

It thus appears that, as usual, the vague horror with
which the religious world hears of the worship of Humanity
or of a sort of revival of Paganism has been partly caused by
the double meaning of a word. The worship of Humanity,
it is plain, belongs to the very essence of Christianity itself,
and only becomes heretical in the modern system by being
separated from the worship of Deity. As to the worship of
natural forms, verbally no doubt nothing can be more plainly
opposed both to Judaism and Christianity. It is even true
that not merely the excess of it or the substitution of it for
a higher worship, but the worship itself in all forms, is
denounced in the Jewish Scriptures. But to those who take
the free historical view of Hebrew prophecy it is not difficult
at the same time to revere its denunciations of idolatry, and
to sympathise warmly with Greek nature-worship. For it is
easy to understand that nature-worship as a practical system
known to the Hebrews might be degrading and pernicious,
and yet that in itself it might contain some healthy elements
which in exceptional conditions beyond the observation of
Hebrew prophecy might take a beautiful development, and

become a necessary part of the religion of mankind. We might without difficulty adopt the idea of a sort of Higher Paganism. Still more readily might Christians reconcile themselves to the worship of Humanity. That which may reasonably excite alarm in these new systems is not their affirmations but their negations, not the new worships in themselves but the repudiation of the ancient worship of God.

And thus we are led to ask in respect to the controversy between Christianity and these rival religions, the same question which we asked at the outset in respect to the dispute between Christianity and Science, Is the difference really as radical as it seems? And again the same answer suggests itself, viz. that these rival schools of religion also have identified Christianity and Theism far too much with the doctrine of the Supernatural. Both alike have inquired what religion would be possible to man if he ceased to believe in anything beyond Nature. They have agreed that all the Semitic religions would necessarily fall, but they have formed different notions of the religion which would take their place. One school has imagined a revival of the original Paganism, which had something of the character of nature-worship. The other has held that one element of Christianity would be disengaged from the Christian system to become the germ of a new religion, while all of Christianity that has to do with Deity would perish.

But however a certain modified Paganism might seem in itself not inadmissible, it is a mere vague literary fancy, which will bear no examination, to imagine this as taking the place of supernatural religion, if supernatural religion should fall. Nothing can be more untrue than that Natural

Religion is identical with classical Paganism, and that to
adopt it would be to revive the "golden years" Shelley
sings of, to substitute a *Madre Natura* for the Christian
Church, and Pan or Apollo for Christ. This is the opposite
misconception to that which pictures Nature as pitiless.
Nature as opposed to the Supernatural is no more rustically
innocent than it is pitiless. For as it is wholly different
from Nature as opposed to Man, so again it is wholly different
from that Nature which may be roughly said to be worshipped
in classical Paganism. When we consider that Greek
Paganism is as full of supernatural personages and occurrences as the most superstitious forms of medieval Christianity, we may well wonder that such a mistake could be
made. But as Greek Paganism is the only religion besides
Christianity which has had any chance of taking hold of our
imaginations, we cannot help reverting to it whenever the
disappearance of Christianity is prophesied. Then as it is
graceful, as we have never been frightened by it as we have
been frightened by Christianity, and as it is called a natural
religion, we conclude by an easy inadvertence that something
like it would revive if the supernatural religion which suppressed it should pass away. But it is a natural religion in
a wholly different sense, rather as not being moral than as
not being supernatural. The fascination of the Fauns and
Nymphs of Greek art, the bewitching gaiety of the Pagan
hymn in the Adoniazusae, do not arise from the absence of
the Supernatural—for the Supernatural is present—but from
the absence of morality and self-consciousness, from a certain infancy of the mind which seems to have been lost in
the progress of civilisation.

It was not the invasion of a Semitic religion that put to flight these bright visions, but the natural progress of human development, giving birth to reflexion, philosophy, morality. And therefore no conceivable decay of Christianity could bring back a primitive way of thinking which had been outgrown long before Christianity appeared. We may indeed, as I have said, admit a sort of Higher Paganism; that is, we may admit that there was an element in the Greek nature-worship which is imperishable. But we may be certain at the same time that the moral ideas which were never incorporated in Greek religion because Greek religion had been struck with decay before their appearance, those ideas of justice, duty, love, and self-sacrifice, many of which are embodied in Christianity, are not less imperishable and are of a higher rank. Nature, considered as the residuum which is left after the elimination of everything supernatural, comprehends man with all his thoughts and aspirations not less than the forms of the material world. Accordingly the natural religion of which we are in search will certainly include a religion of Humanity as well as a religion of material things. It will retain at least the kernel of Christianity, even if it rejects the shell. It will concern itself with questions of right and wrong, it will run the same risk as Christianity of falling into excesses of introspection and asceticism. But along with this transfigured Christianity, only in a subordinate rank, it will include the Higher Paganism, or, in other words, the purified worship of natural forms.

The rejection of supernaturalism then is not equivalent to a rejection of Semitic for Hellenic religion. Rather we find both sorts of religion alike flourishing most freely in an atmosphere of supernaturalism, and both alike languishing at the breath of science, but also we find both sorts of religion acclimatising themselves with an effort in the scientific atmosphere. The one sort may be more sensuous and the other more moral, but both alike admit of being rationalised. Sensuous religion was supernatural in Greece. The feelings excited in the Greek by the sight of a tree or a fountain did not end where they began, in admiration, delight and love; they transformed the natural phenomenon into a marvellous quasi-human being. But the same feelings in the mind of Wordsworth produced a new religion of sense, and this was a natural religion. He worships trees and fountains and flowers for themselves and as they are; if his imagination at times plays with them, he does not mistake the play for earnest. The daisy, after all, is a *flower*, and it is as a flower that he likes best to worship it. "Let good men feel the soul of Nature and see things as they are." In like manner moral religion has taken two forms. Christianity (from which we need not here separate Judaism) is to a certain extent a supernatural religion, but rationalistic forms of it have sprung up; attempts have been made to disentangle the religious principle which is at the bottom of it from the supernatural element with which it is mixed. The religion of Humanity which has been springing up in Europe since the middle of the last century seems the most comprehensive and the least artificial of these forms.

Some such rationalised Christianity then, or religion of Humanity, we may conceive as surviving the fall of the supernatural system. And beside it, reconciled to it, we may imagine the sensuous Hellenic religion. But would this be all? Is it so evident that all which relates to Deity would pass away? Is there not something wholly independent of marvel or miracle in that idea of Unity, of Eternity? May not this also take two forms according as it is associated with supernaturalism or divorced from it? Our innovators in religion seem scarcely to conceive the possibility of this. And no wonder, for if all religion loves miracle, the religion of God must do so in an especial manner. Our experience of a limited physical phenomenon may be some measure of its powers; we may feel sure that we know the utmost it can do. But who can place any limits to Nature or to the Universe? We may indeed require rigid proof of whatever transcends our experience, but it is not only Orientals who say that "with God all things are possible;" the most scientific men are the most willing to admit that our experience is no measure of Nature, and that it is mere ignorance to pronounce *a priori* anything to be impossible. Accordingly those religions which have had for their object the Unity of the Universe, or what we call *par excellence*, God, as distinguished from gods many and lords many, have generally been most lavish of miracle. They have delighted to believe in whatever is most improbable, as best displaying the greatness of their Divinity. *Credo quia impossibile* is a paradox specially belonging to the religion of God.

But does it follow, because miracles gather naturally round the idea of God, that the idea itself requires them and cannot dispense with them? Let us imagine all miracles exploded, and the word "miracle" itself, except in the sense of a phenomenon as yet unexplained, dismissed to the vocabulary of poetry. Would the word "miracle," thus passing out of serious use, carry with it the word "God"?

Who does not call to mind those passages in the New Testament in which—so strangely to those whose faith rests on Paley's *Evidences*—the demand for miracles is treated with contempt? Such passages show that even in a scheme of religion in which miracle plays a considerable part it is not regarded as the only mode of divine action, but rather as the sign of some important change in the mode of divine action, some new dispensation. They show that the great founders of Semitic religion worshipped rather the God who habitually maintains His laws than the God who occasionally suspends them.

The question here proposed is not whether, if the evidence of miracles were exploded, there would still remain other grounds for believing in a God beyond Nature, and even in a God holding communication with us otherwise than through Nature. This has often been maintained, and demonstrations of various kinds, metaphysical, moral, and mystical, of the existence of such a God have been offered. But the present question relates not to any God who is beyond Nature, but to a God who is only Nature called by another name. And the question is whether any worship worth calling worship can be offered to such a Deity.

This form of religion is commonly called Pantheism, but it is seldom thought of seriously. By the orthodox it has been treated as the mere phantom of a religion, while the innovators have preferred the speculation of a religion of

humanity.   Hence it has been left to a few poets, who,
misled by the idyllic associations of the word Nature and
the syllable *Pan*, have indulged in the irrelevant fancies
criticised above.   The God in Nature with whom we are
here concerned is no rustic Pan.   If there be, as we have
held, a legitimate form of Paganism, it does not belong here.
*That* is a religion of natural forms; it is just the freshness
of feeling with which the healthy mind admires and grows
to the living things around it; of all religions it is the
easiest, simplest, most childlike.   But *this* religion is in the
other extreme; it is austere, abstract, sublime.   It worships,
not the individual forms of Nature, but Nature itself considered as a unity.   It may indeed be called out by the
same objects, a tree or a flower, the sky or the sea.   But
in that case what it worships is as little as possible the
object itself, for this religion looks through and beyond
visible things as naturally as Paganism rests in them.   The
infant and the man of science may admire the same flower,
but while the former babbles his Pagan hymn to the form
and the colour, the latter loses both in the law which he
sees behind them, loses the individual in the kind, and the
kind itself in the vista of higher unities above it.   Or may
we not illustrate the difference as well by contrasting the
Hebrew poet's Psalm of Nature with Homer's descriptions.
While the latter touches in turn the sea, the clouds, the
wind, with some bright epithet that marks his enjoyment,
the former instinctively collects them all under one grand
unity— *Who* layeth the beams of his chambers in the waters,
*who* maketh the clouds his chariot, and walketh upon the
wings of the wind.

This worship of the Unity in the Universe is to be found
in most historic religions conjoined with other worships
which are in some cases much more prominent. The
simplest form of it perhaps is Mohammedanism, which not
only contemplates a unity of the world, but seems almost
indifferent to the phenomena themselves, the unity of which
it contemplates. Absorbed in the idea of the greatness of
God it loses its interest in the visible evidences of His
greatness. But in most cases this religion of unity is combined with one or both of the other religions. The unity
worshipped is not an abstract unity, but a unity either of the
physical or of the moral world, or of both. In Paganism the
physical world is not worshipped simply for itself, but a
feeble attempt is made to establish some unity among its
phenomena by setting up a supreme Jove over the multitude of deities. In the moral religions the tendency to
unity is still stronger. Judaism and Christianity are at once
religions of humanity and religions of God, and the former
at least is primarily a religion of God and only secondarily
a religion of humanity.

This worship is not less necessary than the others.
When natural objects have had their due, when virtue and
duty have been fully reverenced, is there not a further and
greater object of reverence, whose existence we must recognise, even though we believe in nothing supernatural, even
though we indulge in no subtle psychological analysis? It
is certain that the thought of a Supreme Being, which is so
natural to man, is not excited only by occasional suspensions
of law nor only by secret unaccountable monitions felt in
the conscience. It is excited at least as much by law itself

as by the suspension of law; it is excited quite as much by
looking around as by looking within.  It is quite distinct
also—this is no less certain—from the thought of ideal
humanity.  Linnæus fell on his knees when he saw the
gorse in blossom; Goethe, gazing from the Brocken, said,
" Lord, what is man that Thou art mindful of him?"  Kant
felt the same awe in looking at the starry heaven as in considering the moral principle; Wordsworth is inspired rather
among mountains than among human beings; in solitude
Byron felt the rapture which "purified from self."  It is a
paradox which will convince few that "the heavens declare
no glory but that of Kepler and of Newton."

Who is there that is not conscious of a feeling of awe
when he realises the greatness of the Universe?  When
from thinking of this thing and that thing he rises to the
thought of the sum and system of things?

But now it is an error to suppose that to identify this
natural awe with the worship of God is necessarily Pantheism.

Pantheism asserts an immanent cause, the creed called
orthodox, a transcendent one.  But how does this difference,
important as it may be in itself, affect the religious awe I
speak of?  That will remain the same, in whichever way
we prefer to conceive the Universe.  The two theories
agree in this, that they give a unity, though a different kind
of unity, to the Universe.  Now religious feeling is excited
by thinking of the Universe as a unity, and not merely by
the particular form in which we give it unity in our minds.

Why should our feeling towards universal nature vary
with our theories about it, any more than our feeling towards

G

human nature? The Man, like the Universe, is a highly
complex phenomenon, which we conceive as a unity. About
the man, as about the Universe, there are two theories.
Has he a soul, which dwells in his body as an inmate until
it is expelled by death? Or is this but a hypothesis, and
a useless one? Few questions can be more important.
Nevertheless, we do not find that those who reject the
hypothesis are as if they did not believe in the human being
at all. Their feelings towards the human being may be
just as lively as if they believed him to have a separable
soul. And there may be a third class of people who do not
even raise the question, who have no opinion whatever on
the controverted point, and whose feelings towards human
beings may also be not less lively, or may even be more
lively than those of either of the warring parties.

It is, in fact, neither the separable soul of a man nor yet
the body of a man that excites our feelings of respect or
dislike, friendship or enmity; it is the man himself; in other
words, it is the unity of all the organs composing him, the
single total to which we give that name. Not otherwise is
it with the Universe. When we realise it as one we utter
the name God, and in doing so we do not pledge ourselves
to the doctrine that God is the Universe, nor yet to the
doctrine that He is distinct from it.

" But why say God, if you merely mean Universe or World
or Nature? Would it not be better to reserve the name
God for the distinct, invisible, eternal Cause of the Universe
which is supposed in most religions, which is denied in
Pantheism, and put aside as an unverified hypothesis in
Positivism?"

This is indeed only a verbal question, for we do not alter the nature of the Object of our worship when we alter the name by which we describe it. Whatever feelings it legitimately excites will be excited as much under one name as under another. Still if a name can ever be important, the name by which we habitually indicate the Eternal Being will be so. Instinctively we attach so much sacredness to that name that we can scarcely bear that it should give place to another, even if another could be found more appropriate. It is the name God which has acquired everywhere this sacredness; it is the name God to which poetry and religion cling, and certainly very strong reasons ought to be shown before we can be expected to tear that name from our hearts and replace it by some other hallowed as yet by no associations.

Shall we abandon it for the term Universe? That expresses—not indeed etymologically but in usage—the total of things arrived at, as it were, by mere collection or addition. But we are thinking of the unity which all things compose in virtue of the universal presence of the same laws. The word World has also associations which render it ineligible. In the first place, it has been conveniently adopted to express the very opposite of what we want to express. The artificial, conventional order which communities establish among themselves—an order unnatural, transitory, and tending to corruption—has been called World, and has been contrasted by poets with Nature and by theologians with God. Even when the word is used otherwise, and is a mere synonym for Universe, it still conveys rather the notion of a *place* in which we live, of an immense residence or house, than the notion

of an infinite Being, with which we are connected as the
part is connected with the whole, or as the member with the
body.

Moreover, it is to be observed that by using these words
we seem to close the very question we wish to leave open ;
for both seem adapted to express only the pantheistic view,
both seem implicitly to deny the other view. It is as if we
were to insist upon calling the human being by the name
Body. The opposite objection cannot be made to the name
God ; it cannot be said that this name excludes the pantheistic view. The etymology of the word Pantheism is
sufficient by itself to prove that it does not. Nor is it solely
in connexion with the theory opposite to Pantheism that the
word God has gained its peculiar sacredness and awfulness.
From the Bible itself it is easy to quote pantheistic language
—" In whom we live and move and have our being."
Both in Judaism and Christianity the word is used for the
most part in the large indeterminate sense. Texts of
Scripture may be quoted, no doubt, in support of either view,
but on both sides alike they would be misquoted, for their
language, as others have forcibly urged, is not scientific but
practical, or—what on such subjects is the same thing—
poetical. Many have found that they received a new revelation of the sublimity of the Bible when first they learnt to
use the word " God " in what may be called its natural sense.

It is the word Nature which science, in its traditional
aversion to theological language, most willingly adopts.
There can be no objection to using it, and on most occasions
one would choose it in preference to a word which, no doubt,
is too sacred to be introduced unnecessarily—too sacred, in

short, to be worked with.    But it is well known to be one of
the most ambiguous of words.    Nature, as the word has
hitherto been used by scientific men, excludes the whole
domain of human feeling, will and morality.    Nevertheless,
in contemplating the relation of the Universe to ourselves
and to our destiny, or again in contemplating it as a subject
of admiration and worship, the human side of the Universe
is the more important side to us.    Our destiny is affected
by the society in which we live more than by the natural
conditions which surround us, and the moral virtues are
higher objects of worship than natural beauty and glory.
Accordingly the word Nature suggests but a part, and the
less important part, of the idea for which we are seeking an
expression.    Nature presents herself to us as a goddess of
unweariable vigour and unclouded happiness, but without
any trouble or any compunction in her eye, without a conscience or a heart.    But God, as the word is used by ancient
prophets and modern poets—God, if the word have not lost
in our ears some of its meaning through the feebleness of
the preachers who have undertaken to interpret it, conveys
all this beauty and greatness and glory, and conveys besides
whatever more awful forces stir within the human heart,
whatever binds men in families, and orders them in states.
He is the Inspirer of kings, the Revealer of laws, the
Reconciler of nations, the Redeemer of labour, the Queller
of tyrants, the Reformer of churches, the Guide of the human
race towards an unknown goal.

# CHAPTER V

" BUT what consolation is to be found in such a worship?
What is the *use* of believing in such a God?" This is the
objection that may be looked for. It is true that the conception of God in Nature, however evidently great, sublime,
and glorious, is at the same time a painful and oppressive
conception to us. The thought of the unity of the Universe
is not felt by all to be inspiring; the belief in it is not
necessarily a faith. For we must look at the bad side of
the Universe as well as the good. The Power we contemplate is the power of death as well as life, of decay as
well as of vigour; in human affairs He is the power of
reaction as well as of progress, of barbarism as well as of
civilisation, of corruption as well as of reform, of immobility
as well as of movement, of the past as well as of the future.
In one of the grandest hymns ever addressed to Him, this
mixed feeling of terror and fascination with which we
naturally regard Him is strongly marked: "Thou turnest
man to destruction; again Thou sayest, Come again, ye
children of men. For we consume away in Thine anger, and
in Thy wrath we are troubled." Bearing this in mind, it

has become a habit with us to say that God thus conceived is not God at all, and to treat belief in God as equivalent to a belief in something beyond these appearances, something which gives the preponderance to good and makes the evil evanescent in comparison with it. If we cannot grasp this belief in something beyond, it is thought that what is visible on the face of the Universe is a mere nightmare. " Call it God, if you will ; but it is a God upon whose face no man can look and live ; from such a God it is well to turn away our eyes. What is the *use* of such a God ? "

But meanwhile He is there. Though the heart ache to contemplate Him, He is there. Can we turn our eyes away from Him ? In which direction should we turn them ?

No doubt, however, many have found it possible to look upon the Universe and see no such Being. They have thought only of each thing as it came ; they have refrained from viewing things in the whole which they constitute. And though others have denounced such Philistinism, and the " disconnexion dull and spiritless " of Philistine conceptions, yet no doubt a certain peace of mind is gained by such modesty. No doubt the religious man will ofttimes be disconcerted, as Robert Hall was disconcerted by reading Miss Austen's novels, when he realises the contentment that may attend a finished secularity, and the charm that may be given in description to a Philistine world. But the contentment after all is a "want-begotten rest," and the charm is that of still life. The mind that is truly awake will perceive the great Unity; at least, if it is possible to remain a stranger to the thought, it is scarcely possible to lose it after having been once enlightened, after having once

admitted a conception which so rapidly modifies the mind
into which it enters.

But is this conception really so efficacious to modify the
mind? Is it of any practical value? Is it not too large
and vague? Or if its power over minds in a certain stage
cannot be denied, if the wonderful effect it has had, even in
its rudest shape, over the nations that have been converted
to Mohammedanism must be acknowledged, yet is there any
reason to believe that civilised minds retain flexibility enough
to be moulded by such influences? The question, when
examined, resolves itself into two, of which only one is at all
difficult to answer. That such a conception may exert a
practical empire only too absolute, inspire a practical energy
only too intense and an iconoclasm only too intolerant, is
precisely what the new attitude of Science shows us. That
reign of Science which is announced in these days as a kind
of ultimate Reformation, what is it but the general diffusion
and the acceptance as a practical rule of this very conception
of God in Nature? Nothing but the vast slowness and
intricacy of the process, drawn out through centuries, by
which it has become dominant, with the constant appeal it
made to toleration as long as it was weak, could have
prevented us from seeing how masterful and rigorous the
conception itself is, and how intolerant it may become in the
day of its power. There is no danger that the new system,
considered as a theology, will be tame or colourless. But
what will it be, considered as a religion? That the religion
of Unity may exist and be effective without the help of the
Supernatural has been shown. But it remains to show that
in the advanced stages of human culture this religion can

take possession of the mind and shape it with a power like that which other religions have wielded in other ages.

Religious men tell us that God, viewed in Nature alone, appears so awful, so devoid of moral perfections, as to be no proper object of worship.

Unquestionably there is some real foundation for this opinion. That God is too awful to be worshipped has been at times almost admitted by those who have worshipped Him most. Prophets used to speak of entering into the rocks and hiding in the dust for fear of Him. It is only because they were able to perceive dimly that which reassured them, that which mitigated the terror and made the greatness less insufferable, that religious men have been able to retain religious feelings. But for this they would have felt nothing but a stony stupefaction; they would have armed their hearts with callousness, and have encountered life with stoic apathy. Religious men have always been in danger of that scorching of the brain which leads to fanaticism and inhumanity. It is not without danger that the brain tampers with so vast a thought, as on the other hand it can only keep aloof from it by resigning itself to a contemptible littleness. What means there are of escaping this danger is a separate question, but as soon as it is escaped, terror and astonishment pass at once into worship. Apart from pessimism there is nothing to prevent the most exclusive votary of science from worshipping. Not at any rate because there is no God to worship is science tempted to renounce worship, but it may be tempted by the necessity of concentration, by the absorbing passion of analysis, by prudential limitation of the sphere of study, by a mistaken fear of the snares of the imagination.

It may be thought that too much weight ought not to be allowed to the declarations of scientific men that their pursuit leads to worship, particularly as such declarations are now less frequently made than formerly. Let us then adduce another proof.

Worship expresses itself naturally in poetry. And again where a deity is recognised there are votaries, there are those who dedicate their lives to the worship of him. Now, is it true that God viewed in Nature has received the homage of no poetry? Is it true that Nature has made no votaries, has inspired no one? Has the Universe always appeared either so awful as to shut the mouths of those who contemplated it, or, on the other hand, so devoid of unity as to excite no single or distinct feeling?

It would certainly be of little use to say, Here is God— worship Him! to those at least who have been gazing upon the object all their lives, and yet have seen nothing to worship there; unless we could show historically that the same contemplation has led others to worship. But this is easy. Ever since the worship of God founded too exclusively on supernaturalism began to decay, the worship of God in Nature has shown signs of reviving. Poetry and art in recent times have uniformly, and especially where they have been most hostile to the Church, pointed towards a new form of religion, towards a new worship of God. How striking a phenomenon is the appearance, since the middle of the last century, of the word Nature in all theories of literature and art!

As worship usually finds its expression in art, calling in architecture to design the temples of its Divinity and painting to embellish them, and invoking him by the aid of the poet and of the musical composer, so, on the other hand, art is never really inspired by anything but worship.  The true artist is he who worships, for worship is habitual admiration. It is the enthusiastic appreciation of something, and such enthusiastic appreciation is the qualification without which an artist cannot even be conceived.  Wherever, therefore, art is, there is religion; but the religion may be what has been described above as Pagan.  It may be a mere appreciation of material and individual beauty.  To become religion in the complete sense, it must appreciate the unity in things; and even of such religion there is a higher and a lower form.  The lower form is that which, while it perceives a unity in Nature, yet takes at the same time an inadequate view of Nature, not including in its view, or not making sufficiently prominent, what is highest in Nature—that is, the moral principle.  Such religion may be said to worship a mere Jove; but if morality receives its due place, such religion is, in a worthy sense, the worship of God.  Now there took place towards the end of the last century a remarkable revolution in art.  For the first time artists began to perceive the unity of what they contemplated ; and for the first time, in consequence, they began to feel that their pursuit was no desultory amusement, but an elevating worship.  Such a thought scarcely entered into the mind of the poets of the seventeenth century.  Milton is indeed haunted by the sense of something priestly or prophetic in his vocation, but the conception in its clearness belongs to the age of Goethe and Wordsworth, and it has had most manifestly the effect of increasing the self-respect of artists ever since.  Here is the best answer to the question whether God considered purely in Nature is an object of worship.   No terror, and still less any hopeless incomprehensibility in Nature, prevented these poets from rendering a worship by which their own lives were dignified, and in a manner hallowed.

Many names from many countries might be quoted in illustration of this, for it was characteristic of that age that everywhere the men of sensibility, the artists, and especially the poets, as using the instrument of greatest compass, assumed a high and commanding tone.   The function of the prophet was then revived, and poets for the first time aspired to teach the art of life, and founded schools.   The greatest poets in earlier times had aimed at nothing of this sort ; but from the time of Rousseau, through that of Goethe, Schiller, Chateaubriand, Wordsworth, Coleridge, Shelley, Byron, down to our own age, poets have helped to make opinions, have influenced philosophy, social institutions, and politics.   But let us think for a moment of the two greatest of these names.

Goethe has always been an object of peculiar horror to the religious world, so tranquil was his indifference to all that they called Christianity.   Not only Christianity but morality itself, as it is commonly understood, was not much favoured in his writings, nor perhaps in his life.   There could be no greater stumbling-block to all who were in the habit of assuming that conventional Christianity is the one form, and conventional morality the one evidence, of true religion.   Indeed so incredible did it seem that a great genius could be absolutely independent of religion, that such persons were driven to the shift of denying Goethe to have

genius. But in the first place it was not to be expected
that a religion independent of traditional creeds and inspired
by no supernatural beliefs would produce moral results precisely similar to the fruits of orthodox Christianity, nor again
is it to be assumed that such an independent religion would
not produce other results altogether beyond the sphere of
morality. We have not yet inquired what is the precise
relation of Natural Religion either to Christianity or to
morality. Goethe is called into court at this point only
to prove that Natural Religion may be a living influence,
and that its fruits may be rich and vigorous, not to show
that they are precisely what we could wish or what we had
expected. It may be affirmed then that the power and
genius of Goethe was intimately connected with his religion,
that his religion gave his life unity and dignity and made it
a perpetual regulated energy of the feelings, and that God
in Nature was the chief object of his worship. Not this or
that class of phenomena, but the unity that is visible in all,
was the thought that possessed him. He felt, as he says,
the whole six days' work go on within him. To know this
by science, and to realise, appropriate, and assimilate it in
art, was his task and his happiness. When I call this perpetual rapt contemplation by the name of religion, I am not
interpreting his feelings into a new language. I am using
his own language; it is Goethe himself who calls it so.
" Who has science and art," he says, " has religion." [1]

As to the attacks which were made upon him by the

---

[1] Wer Wissenschaft und Kunst besitzt
   Hat auch Religion !
   Wer jene beiden nicht besitzt
   Der habe Religion !        *Zahme Xenien.*

pietists and the conventional moralists, it might be easy to defend him in general by denying that the religious mode of a given time and place is to be identified with Christianity or that received proprieties are an infallible standard of morality. It would certainly be easy to show that he had not merely genius but great and rare virtues, some of which —his indefatigable industry, his superiority to sordid or frivolous or envious thoughts—were made easy to him by his religion of Nature. There remains the fact that the idea of duty and self-sacrifice appears not to be very sacred in his mind—rather, perhaps, to be irritating, embarrassing, odious to him. But it is difficult to trace the connexion so often asserted between this moral indifference and the so-called Pantheism of Goethe. If Hindoos have been known to push Pantheism to a denial of moral responsibility, what real analogy is there between their rude primitive belief and his energetic nature-worship? If Goethe thought of God mainly as the creative Artist, and did not much associate the ideas of duty or of self-sacrifice with Him, and if he showed an epicurean indifference on some occasions which seemed to call for energy, there is no such difficulty in explaining this fact by the circumstances of his life that we should be driven to accuse his religion. Many have seen in the moral principle the highest thing in the Universe, who nevertheless have recognised nothing beyond Nature. He who identifies God with Nature will assuredly not omit from his idea of God that which he thinks highest in Nature.

No similar attacks were ever made upon Wordsworth. Up to a certain point Wordsworth and Goethe agree in their

way of regarding the Universe.   Both begin with a warm
and perfectly healthy Paganism.   They refuse worship to
nothing that has a right to it.   Their sympathies take hold
of everything, and with so much warmth, that they have
made the old mythologies intelligible to us by their poetry,
and brought back the days of nymphs and river-gods.   At
the same time they agree in setting the whole above the
parts, in worshipping the unity of things much more than the
things themselves.   Their service of adoration rises gradually
to the highest object, and closes in the Hebrew manner
with, "Among the gods there is none like unto Thee, O
God."   Yet who can charge Wordsworth with laxity, or even
with any alarming boldness in his treatment of moral
subjects?   He is an ardent and at the same time a somewhat conservative moralist.   If it is just to call him a
pantheist, all that can be said is : In that case Pantheism
has not the effect commonly attributed to it of cutting the
sinews of virtue.

It is easier in some respects to discern the practical
working of Natural Religion in such a life as Wordsworth's
than in that of Goethe.   For Wordsworth's life was simple
and unworldly, and betrays under its transparent surface
every impulse that moved it.   We may ask then why the
religious world should refuse as they do to treat Wordsworth's
professions of religious feeling seriously.   "Oh yes !" they
say, "he made for himself a sort of poetical religion," and
they imply that it had no more reality than the conventional
heathenism of other poets, or the Arcadia of modern
pastoral.   Most of them would be utterly disconcerted to
hear him called the most religious man, and the greatest

reviver of religion, of his age. And yet it is somewhat unsatisfactory to account for the religiousness of his poetry by the conventionalism of poetic language, when we consider that he was precisely the reformer who put down this conventionalism, and gave new life to poetry by making it sincere. This writer then, being under a sort of vow to use no insincere language, declares himself a worshipper of Nature, and in the most deliberate manner asserts over and over again that in this worship he found all the satisfaction —the lasting inward peace, the occasional rapture—that can flow from the best religion. He has no happiness, he assures us, and he can conceive no happiness, out of this religion. This assurance he reiterates with a monotonous prolixity, which is natural and impressive in devotional writings, but was likely to prove, and has proved, fatal to his popularity as a poet. What better guarantee could he give of his seriousness? How few writings commonly called devotional have such strong marks of genuineness as these, or are so uniformly clear of the suspicion of having been written less to give expression to a feeling than to give existence to a feeling by expression! And what is there in the poet's life which should lead us to suspect his professions of insincerity? Did he not really rest content with that treasure which he professed to value above all the riches of the world? Did he not remain faithful to his choice?

He may be called the saint of the religion of Nature on account of the unworldliness both of his life and of his writings, which refuse to be tried by a mere literary standard. And why should we refuse to admit that Natural Religion has in this instance produced its saint? To the religious world no doubt such "natural piety" seems unreal; the fixed ecclesiastical tradition rejects the alien type. Not only a dogmatic creed, but either devoted philanthropy or else asceticism—a "visage marred" by some contact with pain —is indispensable to the ecclesiastical conception of the saint. Wordsworth's life was not passed in philanthropic undertakings; he neither mortified nor devoted himself; his happiness was enormous and never clouded. Here again his lot has been similar to that of Goethe, who has lost men's sympathies, partly because he was exempt from suffering. Wordsworth's prosperity was of a much more modest kind, but it was equally uniform. Neither of these men knew much of the darker side of human life. Goethe, we know, shunned the sight of whatever was painful with a care that wore the appearance of selfishness. Wordsworth had none of this Epicureanism; but, accustomed as we are to picture the saint as in the very thick of human misery, as surrounded with distresses with which he identifies himself, and which he devotes his life to comforting or remedying, we do not readily imagine it possible for a saint to pass his life in a perpetual course of lonely enjoyment as Wordsworth did among the lakes and mountains, the objects of his passion.

The type is no doubt somewhat different, yet less different than it seems. Enjoyment was always held to be in the lot of the saint, but enjoyment such as the world cannot understand; if it became him to encounter the pain of sacrifice and to be "acquainted with grief," it behoved him also to triumph over both. Now the happiness of Wordsworth was of an unworldly kind, and if it strikes the eye

H

more than his self-denial, more than his want of wealth and
of success in his pursuit, this is just as it should be, "this
is the victory that overcometh the world." At the cost of
popularity and in spite of ridicule he was sincere in his
work, and he had his reward in the "cheerful heart," the
"soaring spirit," of which he himself spoke. That art of
plain living, which moralists in all ages have prized so much,
was mastered completely by Wordsworth. He found the
secret of victory where alone it can be found. He sur-
rendered the wealth that is earned by labour, trade,
speculation, in exchange for the wealth that is given away.
Others might purchase and hoard and set up fences, calling
it property to exclude others from enjoyment. To his share
fell what all alike may take, all those things that have no
economical value, and that are therefore denied to industry ;
in short, the goodly Universe to which "he was wedded in
love and holy passion."

The completeness of his victory over adverse fortune
creates in fact a sort of illusion as if there had never been a
struggle. And yet there was matter for a tragedy in his ill-
success. It was such as has driven many men to suicide,
many to settled despondency, many to cynicism, and many
to abandonment of their enterprise. But his healthy
strength of heart triumphs so easily that we lose the moral
of the story. We become as careless of the injustice he
suffered as he was himself, and forget the brutal dulness
against which he had to contend, when we see that it did
not affect for a moment his happiness or his temper or the
soundness of his judgment. This triumphant force of
character came to him from his religion. From the Eternal

Being among whose mountains he wandered, there came to his heart steadfastness, stillness, a sort of reflected or reproduced eternity.

Here is virtue in a form very unlike the busy and philanthropic Christianity to which we are most accustomed, of which it is the characteristic mark to seek out distress, and bestow time and trouble upon the relief of it. But it is less unlike some older manifestations of the Christian life. We owe to Christianity itself the story of Martha and Mary. And though the middle ages may have been too monastic in their notions of the religious life, yet perhaps there was something in the notion of the hermit; more things certainly are done by solitary worship than the world dreams of. If work is worship, it is implied in this proverb that worship is at least work. It was not for nothing that our "glorious eremite" sacrificed work for worship ; that the Symeon Stylites of the God in Nature stood there so long "on Helvellyn's summit, wide awake." No modern Englishman has done more to redeem our life from vulgarity.

What the religious world calls mere Pantheism science may perhaps be disposed to treat as mere disguised Christianity. No doubt Wordsworth's worship of the God in Nature was blended with Christian ideas. A Christian faith in redemption and reconciliation neutralised his sense of the evil which is in the world, and preserved him from the pessimism which is the besetting difficulty of Natural Religion. Let us remark, however, that he himself always declares that his optimism came to him not from Christianity but from Nature. He takes pains, again and again, to make it clear that revealed religion does not seem to him to supply a defect in natural religion, but only, one would really think somewhat superfluously, to tell over again, and to his mind less impressively, what is told by Nature. The doctrine of a future life, which he calls "the head and mighty paramount of truths," is at the same time, he says, to one who lives among the mountains a perfectly plain tale. He reverences the volume that declares the mystery, the life that cannot die ; but in the mountains does he feel his faith,—which means, beyond mistake, that the gospel of the visible Universe is not only in harmony with the written Gospel, but is far more explicit and convincing. There may, perhaps, be something embarrassed and confused in the joining of his views, but this only makes the strength and depth of his natural religion appear more clearly.

And yet it is not the "argument from design" which influences Wordsworth, though he may have accepted that argument, and occasionally urged it himself. It was not upon curious evidence industriously collected, and slightly overweighing when summed up the evidence which could be produced on the other side, that his faith was founded. Nature, taken in the large, inspired him with faith, because the contemplation of it filled him with a happiness his mind could scarcely contain. As the scepticism of most men is founded upon their experience that the Universe does *not* supply their wants, does *not* seem to have in view their happiness, so the faith of Wordsworth was founded upon his own happy contrary experience. He has unbounded trust in Nature, because he has always found her outrunning his expectations, overpaying every loss, unfathomably provident and beneficent.

His sneers at experimental science, at the botanist and geologist who invaded his solitudes, are not suggested by any misgiving that his view of Nature will not bear examination. We may think, if we will, that he ought to have had such misgivings, but it is certain that his voice is always given for truth at any price, for unsparing examination. And the example of Goethe shows us that without Wordsworth's optimism the religion of Nature can live. No one is less subject to illusions than Goethe, no one more alive to the painful limitations which Nature imposes on our ideals. He at least does not blind himself, and accordingly he is the passionate student, as well as the poet, of Nature.

Nevertheless this horror of experiment is most characteristic of the religious way of viewing Nature. It is the horror of synthesis for analysis, of life for death, of youth and love for the dissecting-room and the charnel-house. Wordsworth's quarrel is not with the sceptic but with the analyst; it is the paralysis of feeling that he dreads, and not any unwelcome discoveries. He protests against those who would "peep and botanise upon a mother's grave," such characters as the philosopher whom Balzac has since shown us decomposing a wife's tears.[1] For, according to Wordsworth, so far from taking pains to pulverise into their invisible elements the great unities that act upon our feelings, so far from studying to put pounds of flesh and pints of blood in place of friends and relations, we ought rather to recover and reanimate the great unities we have already lost by this

---

[1] "Tiens, dit-il, en voyant les pleurs de sa femme, j'ai décomposé les larmes. Les larmes contiennent un peu de phosphate de chaux, de chlorure de sodium, du mucus et de l'eau."—BALZAC, *La Recherche de l'Absolu.*

suicidal process. We ought not to think of the sea as a
vast quantity of water, no, but as "a mighty being." On
this principle how, let us ask, ought we to think of the
Universe? It was therefore those who had no God, in
whose minds nothing bound together the whole multitude of
impressions that visit us, and whose feelings therefore had
no coherence or unity, that he denounced as men who,

> Viewing all things unremittingly,
> In disconnexion dull and spiritless,
> Break down all grandeur ; still unsatisfied
> With the perverse attempt while littleness
> May yet become more little.

If we see here religion in its fresh untrammelled operation,
we see at the same time its invaluable use. For the higher
literature was reformed in England by this man's fidelity to
the object of his worship. A flush of life passing through
poetry, a new sense awakened in many individuals, made
life richer and purer. His very austerity and monotony,
his want of all popular talent, make him the more striking
as an example of the power of religion. If he had had the
brilliancy of some other poets we might have attributed his
influence to mere literary skill. His clumsiness, what is
called his heaviness, set his sincerity in stronger relief.
What he is commissioned to tell appears all the more
weighty from the slowness and embarrassment of the
speaker.

But for such examples the dignity and the highest use of
literature would be lost. This danger is especially great in
an age like the present, when the state of letters is a very
democratic republic, when the literary Emperors and Prime

Ministers are chosen by universal suffrage. Such an age cannot but abound, as Sainte Beuve remarks of the present age, in literary charlatanry, when it is an accepted maxim that the greatest author, at any rate the greatest poet, is he who writes what the greatest number of people like to read. A kind of literary Utilitarianism sets in, of which the watchword is "the greatest pleasure of the greatest number." The power of a poet is then measured simply by his control over the sources of laughter and tears. Public taste may go very far along this road before it discovers its mistake. All seems lively and busy in the literary world while Waverley Novels and Childe Harolds take the public by storm, while we remark with admiration that *this* author's characters are as familiar to every one as his own personal friends, and *that* author's sayings become proverbs in the general mouth. In the midst of such a literary ferment how pale and cold seems the poetry of a Wordsworth! How dull he is! And how dull would Goethe seem too if only Goethe had not written the First Part of *Faust!* Naturally! Such authors do not care much to make their readers laugh or weep. "To stir the blood I have no cunning art," says Wordsworth. *Ach die zärtlichen Herzen! ein Pfuscher vermag sie zu rühren!* says Goethe. Nor do such authors make it their study to say what the public will like to hear. *Ihr sollt was lernen,*—I meant to teach you something, says Goethe again. They deal not in popular falsehoods, but in unpopular truths. They are attracted by topics which the popular writer instinctively avoids, saying, Oh! the public will never attend to that! And indeed the public often receive their gifts but sullenly. It was overawed by Goethe, but Wordsworth it regards now as it regarded him at first, with steadfast indifference and contempt.

These are the writers who enrich the literature of a nation, who save it from the nation itself, its natural enemy. And to sustain such writers in their arduous course they must have religion in the sense which has here been given to the word. In the long run nothing less than religion will bear them through, though an aristocracy or a learned class may occasionally suffice. But an aristocracy imposes fetters of its own for those which it strikes off, and a learned class will appreciate indeed certain thoughts to which the multitude are indifferent, but not wholly new thoughts, not thoughts foreign to its learning. Religion alone—some absorbing contemplation, some spiritual object more necessary than livelihood, more precious than fame—preserves originality and thus feeds literature. It alone can give an author that happy arrogance of Wordsworth, whose admirers complained that he was scarcely as grateful as he should have been for their efforts in the cause of his fame, so happy was he without fame in the serene temple of his worship.

The result of the movement in art which was represented abroad by Goethe, and in England principally by Wordsworth, is still plainly perceptible both in the art and even to some extent in the religion of the present age. An age which is called atheistic, and in which atheism is loudly professed, shows in all its imaginative literature a religiousness—a sense of the Divine which was wanting in the more orthodox ages. Before Church traditions had been freely tested, there was one rigid way of thinking about God—one definite channel through which Divine grace alone could pass—the channel guarded by the Church He had founded, " As if they would confine the Interminable, and tie Him to His own prescript ! " Accordingly, when doubt was thrown upon the doctrines of the Church, there seemed an imminent danger of atheism, and we have still the habit of denoting by this name the denial of that conception of God which the Church has consecrated. But by the side of this gradual obscuring of the ecclesiastical view of God, there has gone on a gradual rediscovery of Him in another aspect. The total effect of this simultaneous obscuration of one part of the orb and revelation of the other has been to set before us God in an aspect rather Judaic than Christian. We see Him less as an object of love, and more as an object of terror, mixed with delight. Much indeed has been lost—it is to be hoped not finally—but something also has been gained. For the modern views of God, so far as they go, have a reality—a freshness that the others wanted. In orthodox times the name of God was almost confined to definitely religious writings, or was used as part of a conventional language. But now, either under the name of God, or under that of Nature, or under that of Science, or under that of Law, the conception works freshly and powerfully in a multitude of minds. It is an idea indeed that causes much unhappiness, much depression. Men now reason with God as Job did, or feel crushed before Him as Moses, or wrestle with Him as Jacob, or blaspheme Him ; they do not so easily attain the Christian hope. But with whatever confusion and astonishment, His presence is felt really and not merely asserted in hollow professions ; it inspires poetry much more than in orthodox times. It may be confidently said that in this modern time when the complaint is so often heard, *verstorben ist der Herrgott oben,* and after those most recent discoveries which in the surprise caused by their novelty and vastness seem to dissipate all ancient faiths at a blow, the conception of God lives with an intensity which it never had before. This very conception indeed it is which now depresses us with its crushing weight. The overwhelming sense of littleness and helplessness of which we complain is not atheism, though atheism has similar symptoms. It is that very thought, "As for man his days are as grass," which is suggested by the contemplation of the Eternal, it is the prostration caused by a greatness in which we are lost, it is what we might venture perhaps to call *the superstition of the true God.*

If men can add once more the Christian confidence to the Hebraic awe, the Christianity that will result will be of a far higher kind than that which passes too often for Christianity now, which, so far from being love added to fear, and casting out fear, is a presumptuous and effeminate love that never knew fear.

# PART II

## NATURAL RELIGION APPLIED

" *But has all this any practical bearing?*

" *When a religion such as Christianity loses its hold after*
" *having possessed the minds of men for centuries, as a matter*
" *of course a sort of phantom of it will haunt the earth for a*
" *time. Its doctrines, rejected as doctrines, will be retained*
" *for a while as rhetoric and imagery ; even the feelings which*
" *grew out of those doctrines will for a while survive them.*
" *A Neochristianism must inevitably arise, which will console*
" *for a short interval some feeble minds, while stronger logi-*
" *cians refrain in contemptuous pity from* telling them their
" steed's a mock-horse, and they really carry what they say
" carries them.

" *To such pious dreamers the plain English intellect loves*
" *to apply a practical test. To see whether what they call*
" *their religion has any real existence, it scrutinises their con-*
" *duct, asks whether and in what respects they lead a different*
" *life from others who do not profess to be religious, what*
" *religious practices they have, and especially what they sacri-*
" *fice for their religion.*

" *Often this test works so effectively as to save the trouble*
" *of all further discussion. The Neochristian, who was per-*

" haps prepared for argument, if he is not provoked by argu-
" ment, gradually forgets his crotchet.  He does not cease to
" think it true, but he ceases to find it important.  He ceases
" gradually to use its phraseology, because he feels after all that
" it is only phraseology.  The large interpretation, the meta-
" phorical sense, which at first seemed to save the doctrine, is
" discovered after all only to save appearances ; and down
" this inclined plane the passage is made, not out of one
" religion into another similar to it, but out of religion itself
" into the secular life, not out of the old Church into a new
" and grander Church, but out of the Church into the World.

  " Another still plainer test is often applied, which may be
" called the statistical test.  ' You call yourself a religion.
" Good ! how many churches have you built, and how many
" people attend them ?  Where are your missionary societies,
" and how much money do they raise per annum ? '  This
" test too, though it may seem rude, serves to dissipate much
" sentimental illusion."

  Such are the criticisms which are, and always have been,
applied to schemes of Natural Religion.  Let us inquire
then whether the system is strong and substantial enough to
withstand them.  Let us turn from theory to practice.

# CHAPTER I

THE practical question of the present day is how to defend the very principle of religion against naked secularity. It was not so in the last age, when scepticism was much nearer in tone and temper to religion than it is now. In those days the cry was not so much against religion itself as against alleged corruptions of it. It was asserted that the grand simple truths of religion had been sophisticated, obscured by incomprehensible dogmas and unnecessary ritual. If religious practices and ways of thinking, the grovelling fears of the devotee and his servile anxiety to save his soul, were derided, the derision was mixed with respect, for such feelings were held to be proofs of man's greatness and of the Infinite that he carries within him. It was a favourite position that religious dogmas might almost be called true, so long as they were not spoiled by being taken too literally. Much was said of the infinite nature of duty, of the infinite difference between right and wrong; it was admitted that religion deserved all respect for teaching, however imperfectly, these all-important truths, and that much more than respect was due to the great Teachers and Prophets who first awakened men to the perception of them, who first taught that "one thing is needful," and "that it profits a man nothing if he should gain the whole world and lose his own soul."

So long as there was so much agreement between the orthodox and the philosophers, so long as all alike exhorted us simply to do our duty and to believe that in the path of duty—which by some arrangement providential or other was always easy to find—no harm either in this world or the next could happen to us, we felt a firm foundation under our feet.   But what has become of that foundation now ?   Can we gather from what we overhear of the discussions of philosophers that they still approve, even in a general way, the established teaching?   We find that they have analysed the idea of duty in a manner highly satisfactory to themselves, but the result is that all its mysteriousness has disappeared.   They have inquired what it is that makes the voice of conscience sound so very authoritative ; is their conclusion likely to satisfy the almost infinite number of people who feel quite helpless till they hear an imperative command, and who, having lost the Pope and since that the Bible, have trusted that at least the inner voice could never lose its authority?   "The infinite nature of duty," with all such mouth-filling phrases, has passed out of fashion.   The Law of Duty remains indeed authoritative, but its authority seems scarcely so awful and unique as formerly.

And will its decrees remain unaltered in their tenor?   A curious opinion—which cannot be discussed here—is current that when all our religious beliefs have been shaken our principles of morality will remain unaltered.   Nevertheless it is evident that denials of the received morality and revolutionary views of morality have appeared—perhaps only by a coincidence—at the time and in the circles where religious belief has been shaken most violently.  Secularism is in itself no new thing, and its negations might long be disregarded as the result of ignorance; but may they not take a new character when they are combined with the negations of the reigning philosophy?  And on this stream do we not drift down to an ocean of absolute secularity?  Can we not foresee a time when religion shall confess itself beaten in fair argument by its old antagonist the world?

It was in great part by supernaturalism that religion used to maintain the contest.  "You would be right," so ran the argument, "if this world were all.  In that case, to be sure, why should we trouble ourselves?  Let us eat and drink, for to-morrow we die!—*Vivamus, mea Lesbia, atque amemus!* But there is another world!"  And then followed all the familiar proofs, which were not indeed exclusively founded on stories of miracle, but still drew from such stories most of the practical force, the vividness which made that other world something more than a mere possibility.  Are we not then brought perilously near the secularist conclusion when the fashion of thought sets so strongly as it does now against supernaturalism?  Is not St. Paul's argument suddenly turned round so as to tell the same way as that of Catullus?

At the present moment therefore everything depends on the question whether there is a Natural Religion.  May we without pledging ourselves to any belief in miracles or in an invisible, supernatural world continue to protest against secularity, continue to affirm that "one thing is needful,"

I

and to ask, "What does it profit a man if he should gain the whole world and lose his own soul?"

The party which most openly professes secularity does not itself use the brutal language we might expect. On the contrary, it adopts a high-flown style rife with such words as brotherhood. The truth is that, like all vast confused masses of men, this party can scarcely speak without contradicting itself. It cannot be reasoned with, because it holds no definite position, but rather tries to hold all positions at once. It exaggerates selfishness and exaggerates self-sacrifice, and mixes them together in inextricable confusion. If then we would discover any principles of secularity, we must look where we may find them more distinctly and logically stated.

There seem to be two reasoned ideals of life which have risen out of the rebellion against Christianity, which are not mere modifications of the old system but adverse to it, so as to appear at first sight directly irreligious.

First, there is the ideal of the artist. He has long cherished a secret grudge against morality. The prudery of virtue is his great hindrance. He believes that it is our morality which prevents the modern world from rivalling the arts of Greece. He finds that even the individual artist seems corrupted and spoiled for his business if he allows morality to get too much control over him. The great masters, he notices, show a certain indifference, a certain superiority to it; often they audaciously defy it. The virtuous artists are mostly to be looked for in the second class, into which, moreover, it is doubtful whether they have not been admitted by favour. Hence he becomes most seriously and unaffectedly sceptical about the unapproachable sovereignty of the law of Duty.  He does not in his soul believe that the mischief it does to art is compensated by any good done to society.  He remarks the mistakes made by Christian philanthropy, the evils caused by Roman virtue, the homeliness of honesty, the primness of purity. He sides with the Medicean world against Savonarola, with the theatre against the Puritans or Jeremy Collier.  He does not in any sense admit the current platitudes, and he would rather on his deathbed have it to reflect that he had painted a really good picture, or written a really good poem, than that he had done his duty under great temptations and at great sacrifices.  He had rather leave the world enriched and embellished, than do some dismal deed of virtue which perhaps, like the majority of really virtuous deeds, would not even prove a good subject for a poem or a novel.

Next there is the ideal of the scientific investigator.  How much better, thinks he, to have advanced our knowledge of the laws of the Universe only by a step, than to have lived the most virtuous life or died the most self-sacrificing death ! The struggles of virtuous men in so many cases are thrown away ; their active heroism or active philanthropy is only far too active !  How much better if they could only curb this restlessness and be content to "sit still in a room"! As he looks at it from the opposite point of view to the artist, the man of science may think the career of virtue attractive enough indeed, for it has more variety and incident than his own uniform labour in the study or the laboratory, but he despises it as popular, and distrusts its results. All such action strikes him as premature, the convictions on

which it is based as unscientific. " We must understand "
—so he reasons—" more than we do about sociology before
we can sacrifice either our energies or our time to the reform
or to the conservation of any existing system, political or
social. In the present state of our knowledge it is mere
charlatanry to take a part; it is a proof of philosophic
incapacity to allow our judgment to incline to one side rather
than to the other. The laws of the Universe can actually be,
to an indefinite extent, unveiled; the process is going on
rapidly, and infinitely more labourers are wanted to gather
in the harvest. In these circumstances it is a kind of sin to
occupy oneself in any other task. We have nothing to do
but think, observe, and write." And thus he enters upon
a life to which the platitudes current about virtue have no
application. To the student consumed by the passion of
research, right and wrong become to a great extent meaningless words. He has little time for any tasks into which
morality could possibly enter. Instead of "conduct" making
up, as we have been told, four-fifths or five-sixths of life, to
such a person it makes a most inconsiderable fraction of life.
He has his occupation, which consumes his time and his
powers. There may be virtue in the choice of such a life at
the first in preference to one more worldly or selfish. But
when once he has made the choice, the activity of virtue in
his daily life is reduced to a minimum. His pursuit stands
to him in the place of friends, so that he has but few and
slight ties to society. And the pursuit itself may be a solitary one, not leading him to have associates in his working
hours. But though so solitary, such a life may be to him,
if not satisfying, yet preferable beyond comparison, and on

the most solid grounds, to any other life he knows of. It may be full of an occupation for the thoughts, so inexhaustibly interesting as to make *ennui*, in such a man's life, an extinct and almost fabulous form of evil; at the same time may be full of the sense of progress made both by the individual himself and by the race through his labours. And yet, though so peaceful and, compared with most lives, so happy, such a life may be almost entirely out of relation alike to virtue and to vice. Instead of that painful conflict with temptation which moralists describe, there may be an almost unbroken peace arising from the absence of temptation; instead of the gradual formation of virtuous habits, there may be the gradual disuse of all habits except the habit of thought and study; there may be perpetual self-absorption without what is commonly called selfishness, total disregard of other people, together with an unceasing labour for the human race; a life, in short, like that of the vestal, "the world forgetting, by the world forgot," yet without any love or heavenly communion.

Here are two ideals of life which may seem at first sight wholly irreligious or secular. They derive nothing either from theology or from any spiritualist philosophy. The one is a mere enthusiasm for beauty, while the votaries of the other can see indeed an infinite difference between truth and error, and astonish the moralist himself by the emphasis with which they denounce what is unscientific or unverified; but as to right and wrong, it is a distinction they very seldom have occasion for, and which scarcely seems to them to deserve the solemnity with which moralists invest it.

These heresies are not stated here that they may be

refuted. We are not about to undertake to show that after
all the moral principle is that which is highest in man, or
point out what bad effects follow in communities when either
Art or Science usurps the honours which belong to virtuous
action. Much might be said on these topics, but what
we remark here is that such heresies, so far from implying
any depreciation of religion as such, tacitly presuppose its
unique importance, and so far from tending to show that
religion is after all not the one thing needful, derive all their
plausibility from the assumption that it is. For what is it
that is alleged in behalf of Art and Science by those who
take such high views of them? Is it alleged that they are
sufficient for human life in spite of having no affinity with
religion ? Or is it not rather for the contrary reason that they
are themselves of the nature of religion? The artist does
not say to the moralist, "I am as good as you, though you
worship and I do not;" but he says, "It is because you
are so narrow-minded that you charge me with having no
religion. I do not admit the charge; and it is just because
I feel that I have a religion as truly as you, though of a
different kind, that I question your superiority. Yours is
the religion of right, mine is the religion of beauty; they
differ, no doubt, as their objects differ, but they agree in
having the nature of religion. Elevated feelings, feelings
that lift man above himself, admiration become habitual and
raised into a principle of life, a lively sensitiveness when
disrespect or indifference are shown towards the object of
our worship, these are common to both." Not less does
the man of science value himself on having a religion; it is
the religion of law and of truth. Nay, he for his part is

often disposed to regard himself as not only more religious, but actually more virtuous than the moralist. For he believes that his love of truth is more simple, more unreserved, and more entirely self-sacrificing than that of the moralist, whom he suspects occasionally of suppressing or disguising truth for fear of weakening social institutions or of offending weak brethren. It is evident then that if the same men say at other times that they care nothing for religion, or that they disbelieve religion, they are not to be taken as speaking of religion as such, but of the particular religion which prevails in their neighbourhood. The popular Christianity of the day, in short, is for the artist too melancholy and sedate, and for the man of science too sentimental and superficial; in short, it is too melancholy for the one and not melancholy enough for the other. They become, therefore, dissenters from the existing religion; sympathising too little with the popular worship, they worship by themselves and dispense with outward forms. But they protest at the same time that in strictness they separate from the religious bodies around them only because they themselves know of a purer or a happier religion.

After all then the old maxim stands fast, and man has a soul, which if he lose it will be of small profit to him to gain the whole world. For say to the artist, "Never mind the moralists who affront you by their solemn airs; what do you think of the man who neither worships with them nor yet with you, who is insensible to beauty as well as to right?" In a moment he who but now was carping at your language will turn round and borrow it. "The man," he will say, "whose heart never goes forth in yearnings or in blessings towards beautiful things, before whom all forms pass and leave him as cold as before, who simply labels things or prices them for the market, but never worships or loves; of such a man we may say that he has *no soul;* and however fortunate he may be esteemed, or may esteem himself, he remains always essentially poor and miserable." More sublime still is and always has been the contempt of philosophy, which now we call science, for those who merely live from hand to mouth without an object or a plan, the *curvæ in terras animæ, et cælestium inanes.* Neither school yields in any degree to the moralist in the emphasis with which they brand the mere worldling, or by whatever name they distinguish the man who is devoted to nothing, who has no religion and no soul, Philistine or hireling or dilettante. Only in the tone of their censure there is a certain difference; the artist, except when he rises to the height of a Blake, does not get beyond irritation and annoyance; the philosopher smites them with cold sarcasm; the moralist, or he whom in the narrower sense we call religious, assails them by turns with solemn denunciation and pathetic entreaty. This last alone, when it crosses his mind, and he realises for a moment what is to him so incredible, that there are those who "mind earthly things," says it *"even weeping."*

The modern phase of opinion then does not lead to secularity but to new forms of religion, for the systems of life which spring out of it are based on the ideals of Art and Science. Now Art and Science are not secular, and it is a fundamental error to call them so; they have the nature of religion.

Here is the first practical application of the principles which were laid down above. Among the religions of the world we distinguished three as enshrining in archaic forms principles of eternal value, which may commend themselves to the most rationalistic age. There was the religion of visible things, or Paganism, which though generally a low type of religion, yet in its classical form became the nursing mother of art; there was the religion of humanity in its various forms, of which the most conspicuous is Christianity; lastly, there was the religion of God, which worships a unity conceived in one way or another as holding the Universe together. We found that these forms of religion, though theoretically distinguishable, seldom appear in their distinctness, and that in particular Christianity, pre-eminently the religion of humanity, is yet also a religion of Deity. Now if we apply these categories to the controversies of our own time, we shall say that we see the ancient religion of humanity, which has so long reigned among us under the name of Christianity, assailed on the one side by the Higher Paganism, under the name of Art, and on the other side by a peculiarly severe and stern form of Theism, under the name of Science. And when we look back over the history of the Church we see that it has always been struggling with these two rival religions, and that the only peculiarity of our own age is the confident and triumphant manner in which the two enemies advance to the attack from opposite sides.

But whatever may be the merits of this controversy (which after all is but a struggle for independence and for a frontier, since Christianity has never altogether denied but only extenuated the claims of Art and Science), it is but a rivalry of religions among themselves. Against irreligion, against secularity, Art, Science and Christianity are or ought to be united. That which opposes Christianity is not necessarily irreligion; it may be another sort of religion. In that case we may think it false and mischievous, but religion does not become by being false a whit more like irreligion. Nor does its opposition to Christianity prove it not to be a religion, but rather the contrary, as a rival is the bitterest enemy, as antipathy is rather between likes than unlikes. False religion indeed may in certain cases be worse than secularity, as in the religious wars of the sixteenth century the cynic who cared for neither party, even though his indifference sprang from mere sordidness of nature, may at times have been less mischievous than the enthusiast. But whether worse or better, irreligion is always essentially and entirely unlike religion, while false and true religions are always like each other just so far as they are religions. Without some ardent condition of the feelings religion is not to be conceived, and it has been defined here as habitual and regulated admiration; if the object of such admiration be unworthy we have a religion positively bad and false; if it be not the highest object we have an inadequate religion; but irreligion consists in the absence of such habitual admiration, and in a state of the feelings not ardent, but cold and torpid.

What irreligion or secularity is we can best learn from the New Testament, and especially from the Gospels. There we see the rise of a fresh religious spirit in a community, and we see at the same time what is its essential opposite. Not any rival conviction, not some fresh vigorous impulse crossing the path of the new religion, but the want of conviction, the absence of impulse.

The *World* is described to us there, and what is the World? It is a kind of conspiracy of prejudices, or union of all that is stagnant, inert, mechanical, and automatic into a coherent tyrannous power and jealous consentient opinion. *Conventionalism*, indeed, is the modern name for that which stands here for the opposite of religion; and we can judge from this in what way religion itself was conceived, for the opposite of conventionalism is freshness of feeling, enthusiasm.

We may observe that in the New Testament Christianity is never brought into contact with anything vigorous or enthusiastic. No artist lost in the worship of sensuous beauty crosses the stage, no philosopher consumed with the thirst for truth. How such characters would have been treated by Christianity in its earliest days we cannot tell, perhaps with something of repugnance or hostility. But they could never have been classed with those whom it actually attacked, the demure slaves of fashion and convention. They might be thought to be addicted to a false or dangerous religion, but they could not be called worldlings. Possibly they would have been judged with favour, for it accords with the fundamental characteristic of the Gospel to extol vitality at the expense of propriety—those who love much, Magdalens, publicans, prodigals, at the expense of those most honoured by public opinion.

Irreligion, then, is life without worship, and the World is the collective character of those who do not worship. When worship is eliminated from life, what remains? There are animal wants to be satisfied, a number of dull cravings to be indulged, and paltry fears to be appeased; moreover, because worship is never really quite dead, but only feeble, there is some poor convention in place of an ideal, and a few prudish crotchets in place of virtues. Yet a society may live on in this condition, if political or physical conditions are favourable, without falling into any enormous corruptions, and may often in its moral statistics contrast favourably with one which some great but perverted enthusiasm has hurried into evil. Its fault is simply that it has no soul, or, to use the old Biblical phrase, has no salt in itself; or again, to use the modern German paraphrase, has no soul to save the expense of salt. Now it is against this condition, against irreligion pure and simple as distinguished from any forms of false religion, that there always has been, and is particularly in our own time, a remarkable agreement of authorities.

It may, indeed, often appear that the disregard of animal wants and the renunciation of the world preached in the New Testament, are exaggerated. Animal wants in our northern climates, cares of livelihood since slavery was disused, have become more imperious than they were in ancient times, and the education of recent centuries has led us to approve a certain kind and degree of worldliness. Even prejudices, social conventions, and decorums may no doubt be condemned too unreservedly. But granting all this by way of abatement, the general truth of the New Testament doctrine is clearer now than it has been in many ages (so called) of religious agreement. There has never been a time when the necessity of religion, in the broad sense of the word, has been so clear, if there has never been a time when its value in the narrow sense has been so much disputed. If, now that Art and Science have attained complete independence of the Church, and the monopoly even of moral influence is withdrawn from her by systems of independent morality, secular education and the like, we give the name of religion to that confined domain which is still left to the Church, it will seem as insignificant as the States of the Church have been in our time compared to the dominion held by Hildebrand or Innocent. But if we understand that all culture alike rests upon religion, religion being not simple, but threefold, and consisting of that worship of visible things which leads to art, that worship of humanity which leads to all moral disciplines, and principally the Christian, and that worship of God which is the soul of all philosophy and science ; if we recognise, on the other hand, that secularity is the absence not of one of these kinds of worship, but of all—in other words, that it is the paralysis of the power of admiration, and as a consequence, the predominance of the animal wants and the substitution of automatic custom for living will and intelligence, then we shall recognise that it is not favoured but very emphatically repudiated by the spirit of the present time.

If we adopt this principle, that is, if we consider morality to be something different from mere decorum, and religion to be something different from mere orthodoxy, if we consider the basis of both to be sincerity of life, we shall scarcely be so much alarmed as many religionists are at the turn which opinion is taking. Who that has seen the new generation of scientists at their work does not delight in

their healthy and manly vigour, even when most he feels
their iconoclasm to be fanatical? No great harm surely
can come in the end from that frank, victorious ardour!
As for the opposite enthusiasm of Art, certainly we cannot
honour it with such epithets as *frank, manly, vigorous,* or
*healthy;* and yet here too there is life, a determination to
deal honestly with the question of pleasure, to have real
enjoyment and of the best kind rather than the dull pretence
of gladness, the mock-pleasure and mock-happiness which
so plainly indicate something hollow in our wellbeing.
These, on the whole, are movements which indicate rather
revival than decay, rather life than death. For Art and
Science are not of the world, though the world may corrupt
them; they have the nature of religion. When therefore
we see them shaking off the fetters of the reigning religion,
we may be anxious, but we are not to call this an outbreak
of secularity; it is the appearance of new forms of religion,
which if they threaten orthodoxy threaten secularity quite as
much. Now secularity is the English vice, and we may
rejoice to see it attacked. It ought to be the beginning of
a new life for England that the heavy materialism which has
so long weighed upon her is shaken at last. We have been
perhaps little aware of it, as one is usually little aware of
the atmosphere one has long breathed. We have been
aware only of an energetic industrialism. We have been
proud of our national "self-help," of our industry and
solvency, and have taken as but the due reward of these
virtues our good fortune in politics and colonisation. We
have even framed for ourselves a sort of Deuteronomic
religion which is a great comfort to us; it teaches that

because we are honest and peaceable and industrious, therefore our Jehovah gives us wealth in abundance, and our exports and imports swell and our debt diminishes and our emigrants people half the globe. The creed is too primitive! Ought wellbeing to be so absolutely confounded with wealth? Is life but a livelihood? We may no doubt think ourselves happy in not being misled, like so many nations, by false ideals. On the other hand, have we any ideal at all? Does not this eternal question of a livelihood keep us at a level from which no ideal is visible? In old biographies we read of high and generous feelings, the love of fame, the ambition of great achievements, not to speak of higher feelings yet. We neither have such feelings nor yet any bitter regret to think that we cannot have them. We are too tame for either aspirations or regrets, or if we have them we know as a matter of course that they cannot be indulged. Money must be made first, and a good deal of it; comfort, not to say luxury, cannot be dispensed with, for the very thought of any kind of self-denial is too medieval; then comes pleasure, of which we can scarcely have enough. When all these claims are satisfied, the balance of our time may be given to our ideal, if we have one at all; we are perhaps aware that so much will not suffice, but then we are humble, and do not even in our dreams expect to accomplish much.

Where there is the perception of an ideal we may expect to find the sense of a vocation. England surely is the country where the largest number of people lead, for mere superfluous wealth, a life that they themselves despise; the country where vocations are oftenest deliberately disobeyed or trifled with, where artists oftenest paint falsely and literary men write hastily for money, and where men born to be philosophers, or scientific discoverers, or moral reformers, oftenest end ignominiously in large practice at the bar.

Again, where there is the perception of an ideal we may expect to find high and original views of education. Children are, as it were, fresh blocks of marble in which if we have any ideal we have a new chance of realising it after we have failed in ourselves. Look, then, how the English people treat their children. Try and discover from the way they train them, from the education they give them, what they wish them to be. They have ceased, almost consciously ceased, to have any ideal at all. Traces may still be observed of an old ideal not quite forgotten : here and there a vague notion of instilling hardihood, a really decided wish to teach frankness and honesty, and, in a large class, also good manners; but these after all are negative virtues. What do they wish their children to aim at? What pursuits do they desire for them? Except that when they grow up they are to make or have a livelihood, and take a satisfactory position in society, and in the meanwhile that it would be hard for them not to enjoy themselves heartily, most parents would be puzzled to say what they wish for their children. And, whatever they wish, they wish so languidly that they entrust the realisation of it almost entirely to strangers, being themselves, so they say—and indeed the Philistine or irreligious person always is—much engaged. The parent, from sheer embarrassment and want of an ideal, has in a manner abdicated, and it has become necessary to set apart a special class for the cultivation of parental feelings and duties.   The modern schoolmaster should change his name, for he has become a kind of standing or professional parent.

The Christian Church, one would think, is here to cure all this.   It is here, and has by no means lost its hold on the community.   Wonderful is the effect produced by any religious utterance which seems to ring true.   But its system is full of survivals, its text-books have been left too long without revision, its teaching is so archaic as to be in great part scarcely intelligible without the aid of ancient history, while the method of tests and exclusions has drained it of intellectual vigour and has left it mainly under the control of anxious, nerveless minds ; so that it is hardly listened to by men of the world except on the ground that Anility and Puerility after all are forces, and might do untold mischief if they were needlessly provoked.   The religious world, which ought, one would suppose, to cherish the high ideal that the community wants, has in fact an ideal almost lower than that of the community.   It applies the rudest standards, such as the Hebrew prophets denounced in the infancy of the world.   Unblushingly it pronounces a man religious because he practises religious observances, figures in religious societies, talks much and unctuously about religion. "Thousands of rams," as the prophet would say, "and ten thousands of rivers of oil !"   But real religiousness, which, as he tells us, shuns parade, which in fact consists mainly in a quiet devotion to the sort of work which is permanently useful and an infinite solicitude to do such work as well as possible, does not pass with the religious world for religiousness at all.

Meanwhile the great writers who, often indifferent or

K

hostile to orthodoxy, have been the prophets of the present age, have denounced secularity as earnestly as the prophets of old time.    Insincerity and conventionalism have been the objects of their attack, cant in religion, dilettantism in art, shams in society, party commonplaces in politics, in all departments the tyranny of opinion destroying individuality. But to have an individuality is to have an ideal, and to have an ideal is to have an object of worship; it is to have a religion.    Thus it is that modern teaching does but repeat, in these days when it is said there is no agreement about religion, the maxims which have always made the basis of the religion of Christendom—that "there is one thing needful," and that "it shall profit a man nothing if he gain the whole world and lose his own soul."

# CHAPTER II

AND thus in real life, no less than in speculation, we meet with Natural Religion. When we go where the Christian tradition has most completely lost its hold, where clerical influence is extinct, where to reject miracles is a point of honour and the very conception of a spiritual world is at least put on one side, we do not find that we have left religion behind us. We still recognise the feelings, we still hear the peculiar rhetoric, of religion. We find men still falling into two classes, still struggling over something they treat as infinitely important. Among men who profess alike to be materialists one is found excommunicating the other, shrinking from him with the horror of a Pharisee for a publican, and even pitying him with the pity of an apostle for a heathen. These feelings not only appear to have the nature of religion, but they are in no degree weak or faint. On the contrary, they are fresh, and easily become violent. They by no means appear to be the mere survival of an extinct system of religion, but seem rather capable of becoming the germ of a new system.

If then religion is here, working as fully and vigorously

as ever, it follows that we have a religious question.  For in
what relation does this religion stand to our Christianity, to
our Churches and religious denominations?

As the religion is at the present time intolerant of supernaturalism, it has a difficulty in identifying itself with any of
the organised systems.   In these circumstances a plausible
course suggests itself, which is easily accepted by most of
the more moderate representatives of modern free thought.
It is said that the substance of all religion evidently is morality,—"*he can't be wrong whose life is in the right*,"—and
that accordingly all we have to do is to draw attention
principally to the moral part of Christianity, sinking the
supernatural and mysterious element as much as possible.
By this means, it is thought, all the substantial uses of religion may be served; men may learn to love each other;
and in consideration of this grand point gained a little
superstition may be tolerated until the progress of education
shall have made supernaturalism as incredible to the great
mass of the people as it is already to the instructed few.

No doubt it is a plausible view, since there is evidently a
ground of Natural Religion which is common to Christian
and Sceptic, that here a religion might be founded which
should be influential in modern life and yet should avoid
the arrogance of calling itself new.   For it may well seem
possible to avoid the burning question of miracles, so long
as the chief authorities on both sides vie with one another in
asserting that the essence of religion is not in dogma but in
something else, whether they call it "life" in opposition to
"forms of creed," or "charity" in opposition to knowledge,
or by some other name.   But yet in practice the hope is

always disappointed. The Christians on the one side, in spite of the parable of the Good Samaritan, decide that after all supernatural dogmas are necessary, and by the rationalists too the profession of reverence for religion seems to be dropped as soon as it has served its purpose. After all it is discovered that by religion they did not really mean religion. And so the compromise breaks down, and the irreconcilable quarrel between religion and modern thought begins again with no other prospect but of the destruction of one or the other.

At this point it is, at this disappointing identification of religion with morality, that the breach takes place. "Can then religion mean no more than that we should pay our debts, keep our engagements, and not be too hard on our enemies? For nothing more than this have so many temples been built, so many psalms been sung, so many penitents retired from the world, so many saints and prophets wrestled with their own souls, so many martyrs sacrificed their lives? Would that invisible choir be satisfied now with the fruit of its labours could it but see mankind made moral, the planet inhabited by well-behaved people with their passions under control, leading intelligent and reasonable lives? And this result once attained, would the world be absolved from all religious duties for the future? Will the civilised community of the future, furnished with the school and the press, see the euthanasia of religion in the old sense, and look back upon its historic splendours as on the mere transient sunrise of a calm day?"

We have entered here upon another road. In the residuum left after the elimination of miracle we have seen no mere morality, but something which has all the greatness and sublimity of the old religion. Not morality, but worship; not an influence dormant so long as no temptation arises, helping us only in our work and deserting us in our leisure, but a principle of life possessing the whole imagination and heart.

According to the view here taken, too much is said by modern rationalists of morality and too little of art and science, since these are related no less closely to religion and must be taken with morality to make up the higher life. This view indeed regards the very word morality and the way of thinking which leads to a frequent use of the word with the same sort of impatience which the Pauline writings show towards the law. In any description of an ideal community which might be given in accordance with this view not much stress would be laid on its moral purity. This would rather be taken for granted as the natural result of the healthy working of the higher life. The peculiarity most strongly marked would be rather that what we call genius would be of ordinary occurrence in such a community. Every one there would be alive. The cares of livelihood would not absorb the mind, taming all impulse, clogging all flight, depressing the spirit with a base anxiety, smothering all social intercourse with languid fatigue, destroying men's interest in each other and making friendship impossible. Every one would worship, that is, every one would have some object of habitual contemplation, which would make life rich and bright to him, and of which he would think and speak with ardour. Every one would have some supreme interest, to which he would be proud to sacrifice every kind of pelf, and by which he would be bound in the highest kind of friendship to those who shared it. The Higher Life in all hearts would be as a soil out of which many fair growths would spring; morality would be one of these; but it would appear in a form so fresh that no such name would seem appropriate to it.

In history we meet with examples of such Natural Religion. Nations have sometimes their moment when this Higher Life grows so strong in them that it breaks out in visible manifestations, so that they do original and immortal things, and after times look back fondly upon the Golden Age, hoping to revive it by imitation and commentatorship. But in history this appears as "a spirit which bloweth where it listeth," and no one has inquired upon what causes its awakening may depend. Nevertheless this is the problem of those who discuss Natural Religion.

In order to arrive at this view we begin by denying the position that the essential part of all religion is morality. Instead of this we lay it down that there is indeed a kind of religion which is intimately connected with morality, but that there are also other kinds which manifest themselves in quite other ways and yet are truly religions, essential to the higher life of man. From such a proposition it will follow that the plan of insisting mainly on the moral part of Christianity is insufficient and does not meet the wants of the age. For the age calls not merely for a revival of the essential spirit of Christianity, though this too is needed, but for new elements of religion which, though not opposed to Christianity, are yet scarcely to be discovered in it. We shall see this if we pursue the line of thought to which the

last chapter introduced us, and examine more closely that
spirit of opposition to secularity which we see awakening
around us.   In this opposition there is much which does
not seem to have been inspired by Christianity.   And as it
develops and organises itself, we do not see it assume the
name of Christianity, nor even of religion at all; it prefers
to call itself *culture.*

What is this new thing "culture," and what relation does
it bear to the old familiar thing "religion"?   If we might
judge by the utterances of its adherents, it is not dissimilar
nor unfriendly to religion, but somehow more enlightened
and modern, so that it speaks another dialect even when it
would express the same truths.   Moreover, it is understood
to be much more comprehensive, and in fact to deal principally with matters of a different kind.   It is concerned more
with art and science than with self-sacrifice or charity.

This view might be correct if religion were identical with
ecclesiastical Christianity.   But if we take a larger and
juster view of religion, it will not seem to us less enlightened
or less comprehensive than culture, or indeed different from
it in any way.   The name culture will seem to be merely
the *alias* which the Natural Religion of the modern world
has adopted, being forbidden by orthodoxy to use the name
that properly belongs to it.   For it is a general rule that the
orthodox system has kept to itself the vocabulary of belief,
and has thus forced all other systems to appear as non-
religious, if not irreligious.   These systems themselves too,
soured by opposition, have taken some pleasure in avoiding
the old phrases ; which, though in themselves natural and
poetic, had lost their charm, had been stiffened by too much

definition, cheapened by too much use, worn by too much controversy. New phrases therefore have been coined even for notions borrowed from the religious tradition. Thus it was that at the very moment when men began to dare to call themselves Atheists they began to use the language of religious worship towards Nature. Poets were inspired with hymns in praise of Nature, philosophers began to study Nature with a new kind of ardour and devotion; and in course of time through this new worship the old Hebrew sublimity returned to poetry, the old Hebrew indignation at anthropomorphism showed itself in science; and still it was long—so completely was the phraseology of worship pre. occupied by the Church—before it was understood that these feelings were really, and not in mere metaphor, worship; long, too, before the object of this worship was perceived to be none other than He who was worshipped from the beginning, the ancient God, " our dwelling-place in all generations." About the same time, too, when men began to confess their repugnance to theology, their contempt for a science so unprogressive and so quarrelsome, they began, on the other hand, to imagine the possibility of drawing a rule for human life from the new and vast views of the Universe that were opening with the progress of science; but still they called theology their enemy, and did not perceive that to aim at such a new synthesis was to aim at reviving theology. Once more it is worth noticing how from the beginning of the period of denial the word Humanity has haunted men almost as much as the word Nature; and all this while they have pursued Christianity as an enemy upon whose destruction they were bent, refusing to see that

the worship of humanity is as truly the revival of specific
New Testament Christianity as the scientific view of the
Universe is the revival of the austere Jewish theism.

On the same principle Religion has been revived under
the artificial name of Culture.

Thus instead of saying that the substance of religion is
morality and the effect of it moral goodness, we lay it down
that the substance of religion is culture, and the fruit of it
the higher life.   And it is in the growth of the doctrine and
theory of culture in the modern world rather than in any
mere signs of reviving activity in religious bodies that we
see the true revival of religion and the true antidote of
secularity.

Not that the word is a good one.   It is a misfortune
that those who now say "culture" do not say "religion."
The word religion makes us think of feelings, emotions and
convictions, or the acts which flow immediately out of these,
but the word culture suggests rather the machinery of training, art-schools, academies, universities.   Culture is properly
a direction given to the development of life, but religion is
the principle of life itself.   Now it is not by any system of
training, but only by a principle of life that secularity can
be resisted.   Culture again is a word which seems to describe
the privilege of a favoured few, and yet to withstand
secularity we need a mighty popular force.   Nothing perhaps
could contribute so much to mislead the rising religious
movement of the modern world as such a name, which
seems to condemn it beforehand to formality, exclusiveness
and pedantry.   The very word brings before the mind
everything that belongs to the school, the clique, the ex-

clusive profession, in fact all those evils of excessive organisation under which religion has always suffered.

But though the name is unfortunate, the thing realises precisely that large conception of religion after which we have been feeling. For culture is not "mere morality," but embraces a larger field, while it nevertheless includes morality. If we look at the history of the modern theory of culture we shall perceive that its characteristic feature is precisely the assertion of the religious dignity of Art and Science. That German Gospel which the Puritan Carlyle preached to us with a solemnity which seemed scarcely appropriate to it, was an assertion of Beauty and Truth as deserving to be worshipped along with Duty. Goethe and Schiller habitually apply the language of religion to Art, and in the whole school which they represent may be traced an impulse to create a new organisation for the worship of Beauty and Truth, worships omitted, as they held, in Christianity. They turn their backs on the church and study to make the theatre and the university into centres of the higher life. And yet it is quite alien to their way of thinking to undervalue moral goodness, or even to treat the Church, so far as it is the organ of moral influence, with any hostility. In their minds Beauty, Truth and Goodness are of one family; only they oppose the puritanism which sets Goodness at an unapproachable height above its sisters, and they are disposed rather to give the highest place to Beauty.

Their view was probably extreme so far as it was the result of a reaction. But their fundamental conception, to which they gave the name of Culture, is of a threefold religion such as has been set forth here. Culture is summed up by Goethe in the formula, Life in the Whole, in the Good, in the Beautiful. Here Morality, under the name of Life in the Good, stands between Art, which is Life in the Beautiful, and Science, or the knowledge of the law of the Universe, which is Life in the Whole.

When one religion is set up against another there begin controversies and embarrassments. But when the principle of all religion is compared with the opposite principle, when the life inspired by admiration and devotion is compared with the life that begins and ends in mere acquisition, then there is no controversy at all among those whose opinions are valuable. Looked at so, religion is seen to be entirely beyond dispute and to be only another name for the higher life, the life of the soul. When on the scene of history religion appears in some partial, one-sided form, it often works mischievously; again and again a drop of it falling at a critical moment into the caldron of political or social strife has caused the most terrible combustion. It has been easy for philosophers preaching on the text *tantum religio potuit*, etc., to make out religion itself a mischievous principle, and that it ought to be a main object to moderate, if we cannot hope to kill, this unfortunate propensity in human nature. But almost everything else that is highest in man might be looked at in the same way. Nothing troubles social life so much as originality, or political life so much as the spirit of liberty. Of these intractable forces the greatest by far is religion. If only it could be extinguished! In that case we might picture the human family entering upon the happiness which has no history, beginning a career chequered by nothing that could be called incident, and varied only by the gradations of progress, a career the annals of which would consist only of the ever-improving statistics of production and enjoyment; in short, "feeding like horses when you *hear* them feed!" But indeed such a consummation would be only a kind of euthanasia of human nature. It is precisely these impulses and emotions which are so hard to control that give dignity and worth to life. It is for their sakes that we produce and consume. And so it is a more hopeful course to consider whether those sinister workings of the higher life may not be as happily prevented by giving it a full and harmonious development as by vainly trying to extinguish it.

The position taken up in this chapter is that ecclesiastical Christianity has a certain one-sidedness, which has made it oppressive to other forms of religion and has provoked them to a rebellion which may look like a rebellion against religion itself; but that by the side of the rebellion there has been a constructive effort, so that we have now under the name of culture a system which, however imperfect in other respects, is free from such one-sidedness, and reconciles the three elements which have hitherto done so much mischief by their discord.

These three forms of religion have a sort of correspondence to the three stages of human life. The Higher Paganism may be called the childhood of the higher life, and so when continued too long and not duly subordinated, it is the childishness and frivolity of it. Primitive Christianity is its youth, its phase of enthusiasm and unbounded faith both in man and the Universe; this, too, if it stands

too much alone, degrades into sentimentalism.  Science
is the later phase, when reality is firmly faced, when the
sombre greatness of the law under which we live, and at
the same time the limitations it imposes on us and the
patience it requires from us, are manfully confessed; but
this also taken alone is no more than the cynical old age of
the higher life.  For it is essential to its completeness not
only to have acquired what comes latest, but also to retain
and not to lose what came earlier.  Humanity must constantly renew its childhood and its youth as well as advance
in experience.  At the same time that it observes and
reasons with scientific rigour, it must learn to hope with
Christian enthusiasm, and also to enjoy with Pagan freshness.

How different does Paganism look when we contemplate
it in the age of Pericles, or that of Scipio, when it began to
be quietly left behind, and again in the days of the final
triumph of Christianity when it was aggressively destroyed!
In the one case we see with contempt its childish absurdity;
in the other we mark with some regret its freshness and
brightness.  In the great Athenian age a few artists still
with studied conservatism cling to it; and we may indeed observe that when this is no longer possible the great
imaginative poets come no more; but to the majority of
intelligent men it has become a mass of absurdity no more
credible than Brahminism to the young Bengal of to-day.
With still more decisive contempt do the strong prosaic
intellects of Rome put aside and utterly forget their old
Italian religion.  All this seems to us, when we read of it,
neither avoidable nor regrettable; what was absurd could

not but appear to be so sooner or later. But when, after
many centuries, the Revolution has gone much further
when the Church has rooted out of the minds of the
common people what then only dropped quietly out of the
belief of philosophers; when the temples of the gods are
thrown down and their names held abominable; what also
completely new page of history begins, and all such ways
thinking are decisively left behind, some sort of revival of
takes place in our feelings. The new world appears
monastic, too much tormented with conscience, not spur-
taneous or natural enough. We delight to see the old
Pagan fire break out sometimes in Cædmon, and are inclined to wish it had free way, and that there were no Christianity near to smother it. How much we prize what
glimpses we can get of those old beliefs; how much it disappoints us when the writings of those times are silent
about them, and give us instead merely Christianity and
monotonous lives of saints! In some cases we are disposed
to complain even that the native genius of a nation has been
killed by the foreign faith, when we find a literature, after
perhaps a promising commencement, paralysed for long
ages by ecclesiastical influence. Then it is that we see the
other side of Paganism, and what before appeared childish
we are now disposed rather to describe as childlike. We are
struck now by the free zest and relish of the world that
went to the making of those frivolous creeds; here and
there perhaps we see in them the rudiments of a true philosophy. We are angry that this vigorous play of mind
should be brought to an end, and that not by a truer philosophy of nature, but by a timid morality which looks only

within, and is afraid to philosophise on nature at all. In
is̝t, we have just the same feelings as when in an individual
s̝e see childhood come to an end, and the merry, boisterous
t'oy turned into the awkward, perhaps self-conscious and
pa̝:ly youth.

this a̝nce the reaction which steadily and more or less
the hy has for so many centuries gone on under the name
only*enaissance.* It is analogous to the growth in cheerful-
and̝ and healthy worldliness which comes to the youth as he
sta̝ws accustomed to manhood. The self-conscious youth
ir humanity was long and trying. Its Pagan childhood was
ɪrtificially prolonged till it was more like dotage than childhood, and when the new feelings of self-sacrifice, duty,
enthusiasm came, instead of quietly controlling and modifying the old feelings, they began a violent war against them.
One extreme was substituted for another—for the Pagan
view of life, the Christian view heightened by monasticism.
The renunciation of selfishness was violent in proportion to
the intensity with which it had been indulged ; the world
was hated as much as it had been loved ; the extremes of
self-devotion were explored with the eagerness natural to a
first discovery. These excesses are outlived in time, and
youth ripens into manhood by recovering something of the
child. And thus the *Renaissance* is not merely the revival
of ancient arts, the adoption of ancient models, it is the
revival in proper degree and subordination of the ancient
religion. It is the restoration of the worship of the forms of
nature. This worship returns, purified, of course, from all
mixture of delusion, purified from superstition, and, what is still
more important, subordinated duly to other worships infinitely

higher and more solemn, but none the less a worship, an admiration which may become unbounded in degree and rise to ecstasy, and which is essential to the healthy vigour of the higher life.

But manhood differs from youth, not merely in having recovered something which youth had parted with, but also in having gained something unknown both to youth and childhood. Beyond the forms of nature and the ideal of moral goodness there remains another discovery to be made, the recognition of a Law in the Universe stronger than ourselves and different from ourselves, and refusing to us not only the indulgence of our desires but also, as we learn slowly and with painful astonishment, the complete realisation of our ideals. It is not in the time when we are forming those ideals that it is possible for us to recognise the limitation imposed by Nature upon the fulfilment of them, and yet until we can make the recognition we shall be liable to constant mistake and disappointment. The special advantage of manhood over youth lies in this recognition, in the sense of reality and limitation. Youth is fantastic and utopian compared to manhood, as it is melancholy compared both to manhood and childhood. Here again the parallel holds between primitive Christianity and youth. Nothing can be more mistaken than the comparison made by some of those who have regretted Paganism (Schiller, for instance, in *The Gods of Greece*), between the melancholy of Christianity and the melancholy which is the mark of old age. Most evidently all that has been morbid in Christian views of the world has resembled the sickliness of early youth rather than the decay of age. Old age is subject to cynical melancholy, early youth to fantastic melancholy, and assuredly it is the latter rather than the former that has shown itself in Christianity. All the faults that have ever been reasonably charged against the practical working of Christianity (apart from those arising from faulty organisation) are the faults which in the individual we recognise as the faults of youth, a melancholy view of life, in morals a disposition to think rather of purity than of justice, but principally an intolerance of all limitation either in hope or belief. " All things are possible to him that believeth," is a glorious formula of philanthropic heroism ; the mistake of the Church, as the mistake of young men, is to treat it as literally and prosaically true.

Another maxim has to be learned in time, that some things are impossible, and to master this is to enter upon the manhood of the higher life. But it ought not to be mastered as a mere depressing negation, but rather as a new religion. The law that is independent of us and that conditions all our activity is not to be reluctantly acknowledged, but studied with absorbing delight and awe. At the moment when our own self-consciousness is liveliest, when our own beliefs, hopes and purposes are most precious to us, we are to acknowledge that the Universe is greater than ourselves, and that our wills are weak compared with the law that governs it, and our purposes futile except so far as they are in agreement with that law.

This assuredly is the transition which the world is now making. It is throwing off at once the melancholy and the unmeasured imaginations of youth ; it is recovering, as manhood does, something of the glee of childhood and

adding to that a new sense of reality.    Its return to childhood is called *Renaissance*, its acquisition of the sense of
reality is called Science.    We may be glad of both.    Science
will save us from those heroic mistakes of which the Catholic
centuries were so fruitful, from unworldliness ending on the
one hand in squalor and pestilence, on the other in greedy
mendicancy, from pity creating pauperism, and chastity by
reaction promoting vice.    *Renaissance* will redeem the lower
levels of life from the bald barrenness of money-getting, and
give Humanity the *fond gaillard* that may carry her through
the trials in store for her.    We may take sides firmly with
the modern world against the Syllabus, against all unfortunate attempts to preserve a justly-cherished ideal by denying
and repudiating reality, to protect against all subsequent
modification the first sublime exaggerations of the new-born
spirit of self-sacrifice, to banish criticism because it is cold,
and philosophy because it is calm, and to try and give the
feelings of youth the one thing precisely which is most
foreign to them—infallibility and unchanging permanence.

   Nevertheless, the analogy that we have been pursuing
will suggest to us that the victory of the modern spirit would
be fatal if pressed too far, as indeed it is essentially a
melancholy triumph, and that the youth of humanity,
crushed out too ruthlessly, would have a still more irresistible
Renaissance than its childhood.    The sense of reality gives
new force when it comes in to correct the vagueness of our
ideals ; this is manhood ; but when it takes the place or
destroys the charm of them, this is the feebleness of old age.
Healthy manhood must continue to savour of its youth as
of its infancy, to be enthusiastic and tender as well as to be

buoyant. It must continue to hope much and believe much; we praise caution and coolness in a youth, but a few stages on these qualities cease to seem admirable, and the man begins to be praised for the opposite qualities, for ardour, for enthusiasm, in short, for being still capable of that of which youth is only too capable. But in the individual we regard this persistent vitality as only possible for a time. Old age sets in at last, when, if enthusiasm still survive, it is not so much a merit as a kind of prodigy. Is Humanity to verify the analogy in this respect also? When we have learnt to recognise the limitations imposed on us, that we cannot have everything as our enthusiasm would make it, and that if our ideals are to be realised in any considerable measure it must be by taking honest account of the conditions of possibility; when we have gone so far, are we to advance another step and confess that the conditions of possibility are so rigorous that most of our ideals must be given up, and that in fact humanity has little to hope or to wish for? It need not be so if, as was said above, the service of Necessity may become freedom instead of bondage, if the Power above us which so often checks our impatience and pours contempt on our enthusiasms can be conceived as not necessarily giving less than we hope for because it does not give precisely *what* we hope for, but perhaps even as giving infinitely more. On this hypothesis humanity may preserve the vigour of its manhood. Otherwise, if reality, when we acquire the power of distinguishing it, turns out not merely different from what we expect but much below what we expect; if this Universe, so vast and glorious in itself, proves in relation to the satisfaction of our desires narrow and ill-furnished, if it disappoints not only our particular wishes but the very faculty of wishing by furnishing no sufficient food, then humanity has also its necessary old age. And if its old age, then surely that which lies beyond old age. We must not merely give up the immortality of the individual soul—which some have persuaded themselves they can afford to give up—but we must learn to think of humanity itself as mortal. We must abandon ourselves to Pessimism.

# CHAPTER III

THE religious movement of the modern world has been exhibited here as in great part independent of Christianity. But are we not to look forward also to a revival of the essential part of Christianity? May we not hope to see a religion arise which shall appeal to the sense of duty as forcibly, preach righteousness and truth, justice and mercy as solemnly and as exclusively as Christianity itself does, only so as not to shock modern views of the Universe?

This question has hitherto been intentionally avoided. The truth is that if we would bring out the idea of religion as such, we must take some pains to look away from Christianity. We cannot find what religion is in itself by contemplating a single religion exclusively, for we cannot abstract from a single case. And yet much is written in these days about the essential nature of religion, about what it must be to be religion at all, which clearly betrays that no religion but Christianity has been thought worthy of a moment's attention. Hence what is peculiar to Christianity among religions is mistakenly transferred to religion as such. Hence also—and this is more to the present purpose—a wrong notion is formed of what constitutes Christianity a religion.

All concrete religions, Christianity included, are composed of much beside religion. We have seen the essence of religion in worship, and the fruits springing most naturally out of it we have held to be art, science and morality. But morality, if connected on one side with religion, is on another just as closely connected with *law*. In concrete religions, which reflect for the most part primitive, rudimentary, undifferentiated ideas, law, morality and religion are blended inextricably together. Hence mistakes may easily be made in the attempt to draw from such religions a conception of religion in the abstract.

We know that Christianity, like many other religions, has upheld morality by a system of rewards and punishments supposed to be administered by an invisible Judge. But in doing so it has acted not as a religion but as a law.

Undoubtedly much of the power of Christianity under the reign of supernaturalism was derived from the supernatural law-court, as Dante's poem, the very culminating point of Christianity in literature, is sufficient to prove. Nor did this power begin at once to decline with the belief in the miraculous revelation. The Deism of the last century retained rewards and punishments, and Voltaire himself, as his friends complained, could not rid himself of the belief in a *Dieu rémunérateur-vengeur*, that God whom, if he did not exist, "it would be necessary to invent." Nor again is this legal view of the Universe at all peculiar to Christianity among religions. The invisible King or Judge seems almost a necessary part of religion, though in some systems

he is regarded as ruling and judging in time and on earth
rather than in a remote eternity, and in some too he judges
rather the nation or tribe than the individual.   Everywhere
too the doctrine is most effective, if it be not absolutely
indispensable, during a certain phase of development.   The
moral education of societies has perhaps been mainly conducted by means of this artificial extension of law.   In
primitive times, it may be, almost all virtue depended upon
the dread of a Judge who could neither be deceived nor
corrupted, and who punished the individual with lightning
and the community with plague or famine.

Religion in its concrete form being thus usually blended
with a supernatural law, the supernatural law is easily
taken for the essence of religion.   It is supposed that
religion comes in simply to supply the sanctions of morality.
Christianity is often spoken of as a kind of *theologia civilis*,
or useful popular system enshrining the substance of morality
in the half-mythical, poetical form which recommends it to
the multitude, furnishing, in short, the necessary fiction without which the popular mind could never pass from the idea
of legal to that of moral obligation.

But it is not in this form that Christianity is likely just
now to have a revival, since this is not Natural but Supernatural Christianity.   For it is a secondary form of supernaturalism when we suppose an invisible world wholly
separate from the visible one, and so give up the present life
to nature while we reserve another life for God.   Natural
Religion to suit the present phase of thought must be wholly
different from any Deism of the eighteenth century; it must
contemplate its God mainly in Nature, and not mainly be-

yond it.   God in Nature is indeed very really a Judge, for
human laws are evidently a sort of reflection of eternal laws
inherent in the Universe, which have their own ways of
vindicating themselves.   But the future heaven and the
future hell are reduced by this way of thinking to proba-.
bilities not strong enough to drive life into a course which
it would not have taken without them.

The hope of a future life is still strong in men's minds,
and has perhaps been expressed with more ardour in this
age than in any other.   But the legal and penal ideas which
used to be connected with it have almost disappeared.   " In
Memoriam " speaks in every line of a future state, but of a
future judgment it is absolutely silent.   In these circumstances religion ceases to act as a supernatural law.   We
should consider it in these days a mark of low cultivation,
if any one avowed that he only kept his engagements from
fear of hell-fire.   Thus it is with a start of surprise at the
change of thought which has taken place in little more than
a century that we read Benjamin Franklin's description of
the effect which the scepticism of his time produced upon
himself, as a young man, and upon his friends.   With religion, he tells us, morality gave way at once, even to common
honesty and common decency, and it was only after much
reflection that he began to suspect that wrong was not wrong
because it was forbidden, but had been forbidden because
it was wrong.   Such legal ideas now seem archaic, and the
example teaches us to realise—what is now half forgotten—
how potent the supernatural law once was, and that not so
long ago, and upon the shrewdest and most independent
minds.

If this be so, if Christianity no longer enforces morality by those overwhelming visions of a future judgment, the question will be asked, "What remains of Christianity beyond mere morality itself?    What else can remain, unless it be a few majestic discourses of the ancient Prophet who first taught the nations of the West to reverence universal morality ? "

It is time then to apply to Christianity the larger conception of religion which has been expounded here at so much length.    Religion according to this is not properly a supernatural law ; it is worship.    Natural Religion is simply worship of whatever in the known Universe appears worthy of worship.    As to the practical utility and function of religion, we find that it supplies all the vitality of the higher life, or, in other words, that whatever in human activity is free, magnanimous, or elevated rests upon feelings of admiration or warm unselfish interest.    We have dwelt upon the religion which is concealed under the name of culture, and which lies at the basis of all art and science.    But now is there not similarly a religion hidden under morality, and may not this moral religion be called Natural Christianity ?

Conventionalism is in all departments the opposite of religion.    Accordingly where religion is wanting all the higher activities of man are conducted in a conventional or lifeless, mechanical manner.    This is true in art or in science ; it is true not less in morality.

Every one knows how subtle, and yet how all-important in works of art is genuine artistic quality.    In every art the distinction is felt—and the critic has scarcely anything to do but to point it out—between work that is merely clever or brilliant and work that is really artistic. The difference, every earnest critic protests, is like that between light and darkness, almost like that between right and wrong. It is the "one thing needful," this genuineness; work in which it is found has value; other work has no right to exist, and had better be destroyed. A distinction which affects every single performance naturally appears with the utmost prominence in the history of art. Whole schools, whole periods are found to have lost the inestimable secret, and therefore to have left nothing behind that has permanent value; other schools and periods, in spite of great faults, are nevertheless found to possess the secret. At times not only is the secret lost, but the very tradition of it is lost too; it is denied that such a secret exists; and the question is argued with great warmth in the critical world.

In such a controversy the watchword of one side is "rules"; that of the other is "nature," or "genius," or "inspiration." Yet those who withstand the appeal to rules, and deny the authority of the rules cited against them, do not, when they are wise, deny that in good works of art certain fixed rules will be found to be observed. But they maintain that rules are liable to continual change, and that only principles are invariable, or, in other words, that genius makes its own rules; or again that the only rule is to follow nature. When the causes of this difference of view are examined, it is found that the party of rules take a far less exalted view of art than their opponents, that they think of it as a sort of game of skill which is in itself unimportant, but must be played according to the rules or not at all, while the others set no bounds to their estimate of its dignity, and habitually speak of the pursuit of it as a religion, and of skill in it as priesthood or inspiration.    This is the fundamental controversy of art.    In the eighteenth century it was brought into close connexion with the religious controversy by the fact that the same man took the lead in both disputes. Voltaire was as much bent on maintaining the dramatic unities and the *bienséances* of literature as he was bent on humbling the Church.    In the two controversies he had very opposite fortune.    While the Church and the ecclesiastical Christianity of the time seemed almost helpless under his assaults, he saw his opponents in criticism constantly gaining upon him and the renown of Shakespeare looming nearer and nearer.    Before his death the word "genius" had been passed in Germany, and "rules" and "unities" had become names of ridicule.    Nor has the tide turned since. Fifty years later the opposite principles prevailed in his own country, and it is now felt to be impossible to revive with any real success the names of the poets, so illustrious a century ago, who wrote under the system of rules.    And yet in those days Frederick could say, " A *dispassionate* judge will acknowledge that the *Henriade* is superior to the poems of Homer ! "

But now does not the history of morals run parallel to that of art ?    Do we not find the same debate raging here too ? nay, do we not find the same debate equally prominent in the history of the subject ?    Are there not in the department of morals also rules, unities, *bienséances*, and is there not a party which can see nothing beyond?    Is there not here too a genius party, which speaks sometimes of "nature," sometimes of "the heart," and which is distinguished from the other party by a profession of greater earnestness or solemnity in their view of the subject, and by habitually using the word "religion," and with it the whole vocabulary of religion? This use of words is called metaphorical so long as the essence of religion is supposed to lie in supernaturalism. It becomes literal when religion is defined as here. The religion spoken of in art becomes the Higher Paganism. What is the corresponding religion which stands related to conduct or morality as this religion is related to art?

How does Addison's *Cato* differ from *King Lear*? *Cato* is blameless in the observance of certain rules and decencies —rules of grammar, rhetoric and metre, decencies of the drawing-room; the merit of *Lear* springs out of a prodigious activity of imaginative and sympathetic contemplation. Poetry then, it seems, may be of two totally different kinds; it may be produced in a comparatively languid state of the faculties by almost automatic repetition of what has been written by others; it may also appear with strangely new characteristics and only resembling what has been produced before so far as it is poetry, through an intense observation and assimilation of something in nature. To the eye of the true critic the difference between the two sorts is infinite; the latter sort he calls real and precious, the former he passes by with indifference; and yet both are called poetry, both have excited admiration, nay, it was, in this case, the hollow production which was hailed with the loudest approval.

Life too, like the drama, may be conducted according to rules; it may also be conducted on the method of free inspiration, in which case also rules will be observed, but the rules will be different, less stereotyped, adapting themselves more readily to new circumstances, and, moreover, they will be observed instinctively and not felt as a constraint. And though this latter method may easily be abused, though the inspiration may in particular cases be feigned or forced, though individuals may pervert the method to a loose antinomianism in morals, as in art it has often been made the excuse of formlessness or extravagance; yet it remains the true method, the only one which keeps morality alive and prevents it from becoming a prim convention—the only system, in short, under which moral Shakespeares can flourish.

But in what precisely does the difference between the two methods consist? In this, that the one founds morality on religion, and the other does not. For if religion be that higher life of man which is sustained by admiration, if its essence be worship or some kind of enthusiastic contemplation seeking for expression in outward acts, then we shall say of morality that it is founded on religion if it arise out of enthusiastic contemplation; and in like manner we shall call art religious, if it have a similar origin. Now the point of close resemblance between the genius school in art and the anti-legal school in morals is precisely this, that both consist of worshippers, both elevate their minds by habitual admiration. Enough has been said of the worship which lies at the root of genuine art. It is not in empty metaphor that the true artist affects so much the language of religion. The loving devotion with which he traces the forms of nature has all the character, and is attended by all the emotions, of religion; historically, Art has come down to us from the temples of Greece almost as much as morality from the temple of Jerusalem; and when the true artist stands out in contrast to the mere craftsman who makes works of art by rule, he is distinguished by nothing so plainly as by the religious feeling which he mingles with his artistic industry. But let us now consider the religion that lies also at the root of all free morality.

The morality that simply keeps on the windy side of the law has evidently no religion at the bottom of it, but rests merely on prudence. If the constraining force be not literally law, but something of equivalent effect, such as a social opinion or expectation, the morality that results will be of the same kind. It must be of the same kind too if the law is transferred to the supernatural region; the religion that wields those supernatural terrors is not properly called religion; it is but law turning speculative or transcendental. With such morality the higher life is not in any way concerned; but only that lower life whose objects are wealth, safety, prosperity. The higher life begins when something is worshipped, when some object of enthusiastic contemplation is before the soul. The fighting of a William Tell differs from that of a mercenary in this, that the hero has his country present to his mind and his heroic actions are of the nature of sacrifices offered to that object of his religion. And as martial heroism, so every virtue may take two shapes, the one lower and the other higher; for every virtue may spring from calculation, and, on the other hand, every act of virtue may be a religious act arising out of some worship or devotion of the soul.

But now it is not every religion that prompts to virtuous action, for, as we have said so often, one kind of religion bears fruit in works of art.  As virtue can only show itself in our relations to our fellow-men, the religion that leads to virtue must be a religion that worships men.  If in God Himself we did not believe qualities analogous to the human to exist, the worship of Him would not lead to virtue ; the worship of God not as we believe Him, but as we see Him in non-human nature, would be likely, taken by itself, to lead to pitiless fanaticism.

The two great moral religions of the world, Christianity and Buddhism, agree in this, that both centre in the worship of a Man.   The truth is that all virtue which is genuine and vital springs out of the worship of Man in some form. Wherever the higher morality shows itself, Humanity is worshipped.  It is worshipped under the form of country, or of ancestors, or of heroes, or great men, or saints, or virgins, or in individual lives, under the form of a friend, or mother, or wife, or any object of admiration, who, once seizing the heart, made all humanity seem sacred, and turned all dealings with men into a religious service.  It is worshipped most of all when, passing by an act of faith beyond all that we can know, we attribute all the perfections of ideal humanity to the Power that made and sustains the Universe.

The entanglement of these two wholly distinct conceptions of moral religion, that of a supernatural law and that of a worship of Man, is peculiarly obstinate and difficult to unravel.   The truth is that the two views are the more easily confused because to a certain extent they agree.

According to both views religion is a popular thing, meant for the multitude and not merely for a few philosophers. The rules and prohibitions of morality, taken by themselves, are ineffective, but heaven and hell all can understand. And in like manner all can be made to understand goodness when it is presented living and lovely, as an object of worship. The two views also are curiously interwoven together in the system of Catholicism. When we try to explain the fascination which that system exerts, we say: "Catholicism is definite, has real dogmas from which it does not flinch; it exalts and satisfies the soul, which the cold and prosaic Protestant or rationalistic systems leave untouched." This is the language used, but it confuses together two perfectly distinct advantages which Catholicism happens to unite. Catholicism is powerful no doubt because it does not explain away heaven and hell; but its warmth, its poetic charm, have nothing to do with the inflexibility of its dogmas. These are owing to something else. They are the reward of the firmness with which it clings to the true idea of a religion, basing its moral discipline upon true worship, enthusiastic and intimate contemplation of ideals of saintly humanity.

There is then a religion at the basis of all true morality, and we can conceive such a religion taking definite shape and becoming organised. Is this a true account of Christianity, or ought we rather to regard Christianity as being a religion only in the other sense, that is, as a supernatural law?

Catholicism is both together, and both in a very high degree; this is the secret of its ascendency, because with the one aspect it attracts tender and poetical spirits, and

with the other it overawes rude ones.   It is true that
Catholicism has elements which are not to be found in the
original Christianity, for it is specifically the religion of the
Roman Empire and may be said to spring from a marriage
between Rome and Jerusalem.  But if it be at once worship
and law, we may presume that the feature it derives from
Rome is its legality.

Mr. Mill refers with a touch of sarcasm to those who
fancy the Bible is all one book.   It is a great mistake to do
so ;  but it is perhaps a still greater mistake to think that it
is *not* one book, or that it has no unity.   The writings of
which it is composed, allowing a few exceptions, agree together and differ from most other books in certain characteristics.   Certain large matters are always in question, and
the action moves forward with a slow evolution, like the
*dénoûment* of a play, through a thousand years of history.
The Founder of the Christian Church believed his work to
be the completion of the long history of his race, and therefore if we can grasp successfully the kernel of the Bible, if
we can distinguish that with which the Bible from first to
last is principally concerned, we shall stand a good chance
of distinguishing that which is the substance of Christianity,
according to the original intention of its Founder.

Now what in the main is the subject of the Bible?  Nine
people out of ten, reading it with all the prepossessions of
later Christianity, would say, " It is the book of heaven and
hell, the book which teaches the littleness of this life and
the greatness of the life to come.   Other books are secular,
they tell us about the visible world and our temporal life ;
the Bible tells us of the other world and of an eternal life.'

But is this really such a statement as would be given by any one who read the book for the first time, and with an un-prejudiced mind?

Let us consider. The Bible contains the history of a tribe that grew into a nation, of its conquest of a particular country, of the institutions which it created for itself, and of its fortunes through several centuries. Through all these centuries we hear little of heaven and hell. A divine revelation is said to be given to this nation; but it is a revelation which is silent about a future state. The con-spicuous characters of many generations pass before us; to all appearance they do not differ from similar characters in other nations by having a stronger belief in a future state. Their hopes are for their descendants, for the future of their country, rather than for themselves; occasionally they speak as if they actually believed in nothing after death. Then we pass from the historical to the religious writings of this race, the hymns of their temple, the discourses of their prophets. Here, too, we do not soon meet with any clear references to a future state. The imagination of this people apparently does not care to deal with the mysteries of another life. Such laboured pictures of the state of the dead and the rewards and punishments meted out to them as we find in Homer, Plato, Virgil, are entirely absent from the literature of the Hebrews. Not indeed that the belief in rewards and punishments is wanting. The religion of the Bible in its earlier form is, like most primitive religions, inextricably confused with law; nay, it continues so a long time, and no fuller statement of a *theologia civilis* than the Book of Deuteronomy can anywhere be found. But it is

observable in the first place that the rewards and punishments contemplated are all purely temporal, and in the next
place that as time advances this view of religion instead of
being more and more firmly announced is called in question,
and at length seems to be in a manner abandoned.  It is
admitted that the bad prosper at times, and that the good
at times suffer, whether it be for trial of their virtue or to
atone for the sins of others.

In the latter parts of the book the notion of a future state
begins to appear ; it creeps in silently, and seems to subsist
for a time in the state of an admissible speculation ; then in
the New Testament it prevails and becomes part of the
teaching of the book.    But to the end of the Bible there are
to be found no such heaven and hell as are put before us in
Dante ; the writers do not fix their attention as he does
upon a future state.    A few mysterious affirmations about it
suffice them.    We find no descriptions, no labour of the
prophetic imagination upon the state of the dead.    This is
the more to be noted because it is characteristic of the
Biblical writers both in the New and Old Testaments, that
they occupy themselves especially with the future.    The
future is their study, but *not*—this is almost as true of the
New Testament as of the Old—not the future after death.
It is a kind of political future that absorbs them, the fall of
kingdoms and tyrants, of Babylon, Epiphanes, Nero, and
the Roman Empire, the future of Jerusalem, the expected
return of Christ to reign upon the earth.

The popular notion, then, which makes the Bible a sort
of Book of the Dead destroys its unity.    Isolated passages
in the New Testament may be quoted to support such a

view; but it is not a view which brings together the earlier and later books of the Bible, so as to make them seem parts of the same whole. Only by desperate shifts of interpretation can the Old Testament, on this theory, be made to lead up to the New. To those who think the present life a dream and the future life alone worth consideration, the Old Testament prophets, absorbed in their Jerusalem and its future, and careless to all appearance of their own future, can scarcely seem edifying writers, and their religion must seem not merely immature, but founded on a radically wrong principle.

Thus, if religion be a supernatural law, the Bible is not the religious book *par excellence* it is commonly supposed to be. On the other hand, if we take the other view of religion which has been presented here, we shall find that of *this* religion the Bible is the text-book as no other book is or can be. Do we want an idea which shall give unity to the Bible, which shall make Old Testament and New and the separate writings composing both seem—in the main and roughly, for more is not to be expected—to belong together and to make up a great whole? Just as clearly as the idea of a future life is not this, the idea of morality inspired and vivified by religion in the manner above described is this. The idea of a future life is one which we ourselves read into the Bible; the idea which we find there, pervading it from first to last, is one which belongs altogether to practical life, and which must seem just as important to the sceptic as to the most believing supernaturalist; it is the idea summed up in an antithesis which takes many forms, the antithesis of letter and spirit, law and grace, works and faith.

When we consider human action, whether theoretically or historically, we are always brought back to this fundamental antithesis.   Human action is either mechanical or intelligent, either conventional or rational.   Either it follows custom or reason, either it is guided by rules or by inspiration.   In morals as in poetry you must be of the school either of Boileau or of Shakespeare.   Either you must sedulously observe a number of regulations you do not hope to understand, or you must move freely towards an end you passionately conceive, at times making new rules for yourself, at times rejecting old ones, and allowing to convention only a kind of provisional or presumptive validity.   The greatness of the Bible, its title to be called the Book *par excellence* lies in this, that it grasps firmly this fundamental antithesis, expounds and illustrates it exhaustively through a history of many centuries, and leaves it in the act of revolutionising the world.   It thus becomes the unique Epic of Human Action, the Book of Dead and Living Morality.

We associate this controversy of works and faith principally with the name of St. Paul and with that last chapter of the Biblical history in which a national creed was generalised, so as to be capable of becoming the religion of the Roman Empire.   But in reality the fifth act of the drama does not differ from the earlier acts, for the drama is one.   That earlier rebellion against the authority of Scribes and Pharisees was, from the present point of view, another aspect of the same controversy.   It was parallel to those transitions in literature or art when the commentatorial spirit is renounced, when free inspiration moves again, the yoke of authority is broken, and new leaders assert their equality or superiority to the most venerated names of the past. So too of the prophetic movement of the old Monarchy. It is an effort to put life into a mass of usages and ceremonies. Statutes, ordinances, ceremonies, are brooded on till the mind of the lawgiver is thought to be discerned in them. Then when the system has been in this manner verified, a principle of progress begins to work, new obligations are discovered, new statutes seem to issue from the invisible Source of authority, until morality is set free from law and begins to be independent of rewards and punishments. Nor is the subject handled in a one-sided or fanatical spirit. It is recognised not only that the stereotyped letter is valuable, not only that it is to be protected at any sacrifice against foreign admixtures, and guarded with watchful zeal against neglect, but it is also admitted, even by the leading champions of freedom, that there is a period or stage of national life when law is predominant, that the law is a pedagogue, and the like. And thus the transition, in which Ezra takes the lead, is in favour of the most punctilious legality, and a long period follows, in which the commentatorial spirit rules, and the stream of inspiration runs shallower, until it dries up altogether.

When a great number of documents in different styles and of different periods are presented to a reader as one book, nothing is more natural than that he should miss the clue to such a book, and find it difficult to distinguish what is episodical or accidental in it from what belongs to the main subject. Thus some readers of the Bible fix upon its revelations of a future state, and overlook the striking silence about a future state which most of the Biblical books preserve; others fix upon its miracles, though it is easy to quote from the New Testament passages in which the evidence of miracles is spoken of slightingly.  Sceptics deny that the Bible has any unity at all, and no doubt we cannot without assuming a miracle think to discover in the Bible the same degree of unity as in a single treatise.  But each genuine national literature, compared with other literatures, has a certain unity, and in Israel national consciousness was intense.  What we find, if we read without prepossession, is precisely what we should expect.  We find a history of the nation much more intense and ideal than other histories, in which therefore the fundamental lesson of history is more successfully brought out, in which it is shown how law disciplines those who are subject to it, until, after a long course of generations, there springs up a morality which is free, active, and energetic, because it is founded upon the religion of ideal humanity.

We find then no "mere morality," but a historical religion with its classical literature.  The influence of the Greek and Latin classics is not now less than it was, perhaps it is even greater; and yet criticism has cancelled some centuries of the history of Greece and Rome as untrustworthy, and has denied the personality of Homer, while the authority of Aristotle has been long since renounced in the schools and in the theatre, new sciences and literatures have sprung up, and the last traces of the Roman Empire have disappeared from the system of Europe.  Just as indestructible by criticism or changes of opinion will the influence of the Hebrew classics prove; and that which is peculiar to the Bible, and has caused it to be spoken of as one book rather than many, viz. the unity reigning through a work upon which so many generations laboured, gives it a vastness beyond comparison, so that the greatest work of individual literary genius shows by the side of it like some building of human hands beside the Peak of Teneriffe.

There are some now living who after passing through all the religious perplexities of their age, after doubting whatever can be doubted, all that the Churches call orthodoxy and all the supernatural claims that have been made for the Bible, yet believe in the Bible more than ever.  They brood on it much more, they learn from it much more, than they did while they were afraid to suffer their minds to play upon its contents.  Nor do they regard it merely as a historic document, valuable for the light it throws on the growth of religious ideas but obsolete as a practical manual. They find in it the same intense vitality as in some Greek books, the vitality breathed from one of the small antique states.  They find the old Jewish society in its hunger for righteousness going deeper into the secrets of practical ethics than the modern world goes, just as they find the modern world surpassed by Athens and Florence in the sense for art.

It is thus that we arrive at a Christianity which is independent of supernaturalism but at the same time is historic not abstract, and does not in any way break with the Christian tradition or discard the Christian documents as obsolete.  The miracles of the Bible, if the world should ultimately decide to reject them, would fall away, and in doing so would undoubtedly damage the orthodox system. But the Natural Christianity sketched in this chapter would not be damaged. They would damage also the Bible considered as a Koran or Sibylline Book, but as a classical literature and a history of the religion hidden under morality it would not be damaged, as the legendary element in the . Greek literature does not diminish but perhaps rather enhances its value.

Let us not, however, blink the fact that classical books too may be abused. Thus we may sincerely acknowledge the inestimable benefit that comes from the kind of consecration which the Greek and Latin writers have received, and yet we may hold that the study of the classics keeps artificially alive a great deal of obsolete sentiment. It is not every reader of an ancient book that can make the proper allowance for the lapse of two thousand years. This drawback, we ought to admit, is more serious in the case of the Bible than in that of the Greek and Latin classics in proportion as the Bible is more universally circulated and takes a stronger hold. The reader takes every word as addressed to himself, whereas the first condition of understanding it rightly is to be alive to the fact that it was addressed to wholly different people living in a different period of history. Hence the wildest mistakes are made, and in every country in which the Bible is universally read a large proportion of the people is a prey to dangerous hallucinations which sometimes disfigure the page even of public history, as in the chapter of our Commonwealth.

Moreover, the Bible is a fragment, and standing alone creates an illusion which has incalculable bad results. The grand ideal narrative by stopping short suddenly conveys an impression as if revelation itself had ceased and the world had since lived under a different and less divine law.   Or if a later generation attempt, like the Puritans, to rise once more to the same general view of human affairs, they fail, because they have no clue to the centuries immediately behind them, of which no Bible has been written.

If the struggle between two sorts of morality recorded there be really so fundamental and universal wherever human beings pretend to any morality as we have represented it, evidently the record ought to be continued so as to embrace modern times.   It ought to be related how the free morality, after being successfully revealed to the world, became the religion of races which were so far from being ripe for it, that they were but just ready for the legal stage; and how of necessity a new system of Christian legalism arose which reigned for centuries; how, after disciplining a barbarian world, this system, so powerful, though so radically self-contradictory, gave way, and the language of St. Paul about faith and liberty began to be intelligible again; how the tyranny of a church gave place to the less intolerable tyranny of a book, while the nations were preparing themselves to take up once again the freedom of those who live not by rules but by religion, the religion of ideal humanity.

# CHAPTER IV

## NATURAL RELIGION AND THE STATE

NATURAL Religion then is no mere dull morality, for in the first place it is far wider than any morality, being as wide as modern culture, and in the second place so far as it is moral and bears fruit in morality, even here it is no mere morality, but a historic religion of humanity. A true religious life then—so much perhaps has been shown to be possible without aid from supernaturalism. But a new objection makes itself heard. "Possible to whom? To a few elect spirits more finely gifted than the average of mankind, or to a few fortunate people lifted above common cares and rich enough to indulge in spiritual luxuries? But religion in the proper sense is no such delicate thing. Either it is one of the great forces which sway whole communities at once, or it is nothing. We may speak with all respect of those refined systems which find an adherent here and there among the thoughtful few, but we should call them philosophy rather than religion. And of this kind is every variety of rationalism, every system of belief which excludes the supernatural. In their place such systems may be respectable, but they wear a disguise when they present themselves in the character of religion."

In the ecclesiastical world Natural Religion is commonly hooted down with a confused clamour of Mere morality! Mere philosophy! as though these two contemptuous epithets had much the same meaning. But there is a great difference between them. The charge of Mere morality! has been examined, but it remains to meet those who cry Mere philosophy! Natural Religion may be much more than a mere morality, it may satisfy and elevate the soul as no dead morality can do, but it may lack nevertheless all popular power, it may be a mere philosophy, incurably cold and incomprehensible to the mass of mankind.

It is said that the theophilanthropist Larevellière-Lepeaux once confided to Talleyrand his disappointment at the ill-success of his attempt to bring into vogue a sort of improved Christianity, a benevolent rationalism which he had invented to meet the wants of a sceptical age. "His propaganda made no way," he said; "what was he to do?" he asked. The ex-bishop politely condoled with him, feared it was indeed a difficult task to found a new religion, more difficult than could be imagined, so difficult that he hardly knew what to advise! "Still"—so he went on after a moment's reflection—"there is one plan which you might at least try; I should recommend you *to be crucified and to rise again the third day.*"

Yes, indeed! this is a lightning-flash that clears the air. It reminds us what religion was in the days when religion was strong, what a robust unmistakable thing, and how helplessly languid are these modern imitations of it. It shows us how they strike a statesman who has been accustomed to respect the old genuine religion and to make Concordats with it, but perceives at once that the modern religion will never demand a Concordat.

The great religions of the world have been mighty social and political forces. Often, as has been said above, they have been but law under a disguise; in these cases naturally they have been closely connected with the organisation of states. It has been laid down here that in the sense of a supernatural law religion is not likely to revive in the modern world. The question now is whether it follows from this admission that religion is henceforth to have no commanding influence upon society at large or upon public affairs.

Before we inquire whether Natural Religion may be expected to show this kind of commanding power, it will be necessary to ask ourselves whether we should desire it to do so. For indeed though we are in general disposed to respect religion and to regret the decline of it, yet we have in our minds a mild and somewhat feeble type. A strong religion, when it is clearly put before us, causes us to shrink back with alarm. Something more, no doubt, than a mere philosophy, some sort of Church we are prepared to expect —for surely every variety of religious opinion must have its organised society, the most isolated schismatic must at least have his congregation—but we are equally convinced that it is the first duty of a Church to be humble, modest, rather insignificant, to pretend to no public character, to shrink with a kind of horror from all connexion with politics. " Religion," so runs the maxim, " is an affair between man and his Maker." The modern view is that the State is the legitimate authority, to which alone belongs the right of exacting obedience, but that under the shield of the State, wholly separate from it and regarded by it with cold impartiality, there may probably exist modest societies in which those who hold common opinions on moral and religious subjects may meet for edification. This is a practical view, the result of much bitter experience of the excesses into which concrete religions have fallen when they have had uncontrolled power. The maxim that "religion is an affair between man and his Maker" has assuredly done a world of good, and it has also an impressive sound.

But is it true? For it seems almost easier to believe that religion is a mischievous thing than that it is a good thing and yet requires to be so carefully diluted. Does history exhibit religion as such a secondary influence, as rendering such very humble unobtrusive services to mankind?

We may think so as long as we follow what is the received method in religious discussion, treating Christianity as the only religion worthy of notice, and every other religion as simply a hateful imposture. For this method confines our view absolutely to the history of the Christian Church. It teaches us, for instance, to put aside without the least hesitation the example of complete union of Church and State presented by Judaism, and never even to recollect other examples presented by heathen forms of religion. In Christian history taken alone we do not, to be sure, find the weight of evidence decidedly in favour of the modern view. On the contrary, for twelve centuries out of eighteen the Christian Church was in close connexion with the European States, and in those centuries in which Christianity appears to the historian most mighty and beneficent, when she was gathering barbarous nations into the fold of civilisation, the Church eclipsed and tended to absorb the State. But this serious fact is supposed to be outweighed by the agreement of the latest and most civilised with the earliest and purest ages of Christianity in favour of a more retiring kind of religion. The primitive Church was a modest society in the bosom of an imperious State, and such has the modern Church since the eighteenth century under the light of civilisation and science tended once more to become.

This consideration in itself seems hardly conclusive. The twelve theocratic centuries of Christianity may be thought to show its essential character more truly than either those which came before or those which have followed, because they offered fewer obstacles to its development. If in the first ages its sphere was narrow, this was evidently because it had not yet bulk and substance enough for a larger one ; it assumed power as soon as it was able to do so. Nor did it begin to abandon this power again until it had become weakened by division, for the plan of relegating religion to the private sphere did not begin to be adopted till the Reformation had introduced two Christianities where there had been but one before.

But if we look beyond Christianity and form our idea of religion by a comparison of the different forms it has assumed, we shall be much more struck by its social character and the organising power which it exerts wherever it is powerful at all. Nay, more, we shall find that the contrast we make between Church and State, as if they were two independent

and rival organisations, is scarcely historical and is founded
upon a very special experience. History does not confirm
the notion that men form one organisation for secular
purposes and another for spiritual union, and that these two
organisations afterwards enter into rivalry. Rather it shows
us religion as the principal influence by which men are
organised in the communities which afterwards ripen into
states. Alliance and still more rivalry between Church and
State are late and accidental developments; in the ordinary
case the human community may be called almost indifferently
by the name State or Church, though in the earliest periods
the name Church and in the latest the name State seems
usually most appropriate. Nor is this purely a primitive
phase of society, interesting only to students; nor again
does it seem so clear that in civilised times it necessarily
gives place to a wholly different phase, in which the State is
supreme and purely secular, but allows the existence of
modest and insignificant religious associations.

That primitive phase itself it is easy for us all to realise,
because we know by heart the hymns of the old Jewish
religion. We can measure the intimate union of Church
and State in Israel by remarking the religious character
which belongs in that literature to such words as Jerusalem
and Zion. The name of a City there suggests not so much
law-courts, or even a king's palace, as the home of a God.
To us it would be startling if the name England were
introduced in our hymns or sung in our churches. What
should we think then if its name and its glories formed the
staple of our religious worship, if our church-goers sang—
"O pray for the peace of England—they shall prosper that

N

love thee.   God is in the midst of her, she shall not be
moved. . . . Walk about—and go round about her and tell
the towers thereof. . . . For this God is our God for ever
and ever"?   But it may be answered by one party that
Jerusalem really was a sacred place but that England is not,
and by an opposite school that the Jews were fanatics whose
devotion to their own institutions caused their own ruin and
misled the world.   Let us go then to the home of philosophy
and art, to Athens.   Do we suppose that Church and State
were separated there, that the patriotism of the heroes of
Marathon and Salamis was a purely secular feeling, that they
were inspired not by feelings of religion but by rational
considerations of the indispensable value of democracy to
mankind?   Fortunately the voice of one of the generation
of the Μαραθωνομάχαι is still heard among mankind.   To
Aeschylus Athens is the place where Athena comes to sit
personally in judgment and preside over the balloting of the
jurors, where the Eumenides have been propitiated and
condescend to live among the citizens in their sacred cavern.
Not less in the mind of Sophocles are religion and patriotism
indistinguishably blended.   In his ideal picture of Athens
which breathes such an exquisite tenderness it is not institutions, new improvements or the like, that he dwells on, but
the presence of Gods.   Titan Prometheus "has" one district;
the neighbouring fields look up to the horseman Colonus,
and the whole is watched by the ever-seeing orb of Morian
Jove and by Athena.   Athena! yes, the Athenian scarcely
knows whether he is named after his goddess or his City;
when his mind dwells upon Athens, it dwells first and
principally upon the Power which makes its abode there.

All this no doubt is primitive in its form; but are we right when we imagine that a new kind of religion wholly different and of an essentially personal and private character has since been introduced? Is it true that whereas the ancient religions including the Jewish were closely connected with public and national life, Christianity is different in kind, being purely of the nature of a philosophy and intended only as a guide to the individual conscience? It has no doubt occasionally taken this character, but all religions alike must do so in certain adverse circumstances. The homogeneous community which is State and Church at once may cease to be possible. This will happen, for instance, when such communities are blended or confused together by conquest, as in the Roman Empire; it will happen again, as in modern Europe, when the natural unforced consent of opinion which the old religions required has been destroyed by schism and scepticism. Then will appear the phenomenon of private religion, scarcely distinguishable from philosophy but capable of being represented as pure and innocent just because it is weak. It does not appear that Christianity has ever wished or consented, except under constraint, to be such a religion. Its nature is misrepresented when it is reduced to a set of philosophical or quasi-philosophical opinions, its history is misrepresented when it is described as a quiet spiritual influence, wholly removed from the turmoil of public disturbances, and spreading invisibly from heart to heart. Its rise and success are closely connected with great political revolutions. It springs up in the bosom of a primitive state-church or church-state; its birth-throes are like a nationality move-

ment, like the beginning of a war of liberation, so much so
that its Founder is charged with rebellion.   Its earliest controversy concerns the question of nationality; not opinions
or dogmas but the acceptance of the badge of a particular
nation, this is the first test we hear of in the history of
Christianity.   And when we take a broad view of the
gradual rise of this religion to universal dominion we do
not find it making its way after the fashion of a scientific
discovery, but we see it taking advantage of peculiar circumstances in the composition of the Roman Empire.   One of
these circumstances was the wide diffusion of the Jewish
nationality, which helped the new doctrine into notice
everywhere at once.   Another was the hopeless decay of
Roman religion and the difficulty of holding the Empire
together without the help of a great spiritual force.   For in
spite of the striking ability with which the Roman adminis-
trators applied the conception of a purely secular system
which should be only a State and should contain Churches
without being a Church, the experiment did not in the end
succeed.   The Roman Empire became in its turn by the
acceptance of Christianity, what ancient Israel and ancient
Athens had been, a city of God.   Most instructive is it to
trace the process by which amid the terrible storms of the
fifth century this change was thoroughly consolidated, the
curious compromise between the Roman Empire and the
Christian Church by which Rome became the sacred centre
of a religion which had at the beginning regarded Rome
with abhorrence, the strange composite religion which was
made by blending Christian ideas with Roman maxims so
as to oppose to the inroad of barbarism the essence of

ancient civilisation concentrated into a creed. The final result was the Holy Roman Empire, a Charles crowned by the Church, and standing forth in the attitude of David as the head of a European theocracy.

Thus the first great experiment of a purely secular State had failed. After this men lived once more for centuries in one of those spiritual fabrics which are State and Church alike, and this time on a vast universal scale. Then in its turn the theocratic Roman Empire decayed, though even now it remains the most conspicuous fact about the Christian Church that the name of the world-state Rome is stamped upon the largest branch of it. But the Roman Church stands there isolated and scarcely intelligible to the modern world because it has lost the Roman Empire to which it belongs. States founded on a different principle, national States, have arisen on the territory of the universal State, and the national States in their turn strove for a long time to be Cities of God. In the seventeenth century Scotland reproduced all the characteristics and accustomed itself to the phrases of the Jewish theocracy, and the world saw again a covenanted people.

Even the French Revolution conceived religion as public. It made two experiments in religion. At first the Church was to be Christian and Gallican. This was the aim of the Constitution Civile. When the times grew wilder Christianity was renounced, but the idea of a national religion, some worship of the Supreme Being or the Country, grounded on the theocratic views of Rousseau, lingered in the French mind. Since then, however, we have witnessed a powerful revival of the secular State, as it was seen in the earlier

Roman Empire, and nothing henceforth can be more unlikely than any revival of the old type of public religion. But what was that old type? For we are to remember that religion may be conceived either as a law or as a worship. Now it is as a law that public religion is declining; not only have the punishments of a future state lost much of their deterrent influence, but "courts Christian" in this life, the whole machinery of religious law, everything that connects religion as such with the magistrate, is in the course of being exploded.

But religion in the other sense remains. In this sense may it not continue to be public and all-embracing? Or must we needs allow religion to be lost in the crowd of tenable opinions and to become a mere philosophy? The advocates of the secular state and the private religion are unwilling to acknowledge that they do this. They point to the primitive Church, and they argue that their voluntary churches are no more like mere philosophic schools than the voluntary independent churches of Corinth and Ephesus were like the philosophic schools that may have flourished beside these. That age, they tell us, was the purest age of the Church; we can desire nothing better than to restore it. Let Truth confide in her own weapons; she will certainly prevail.

Prevail! yes, but when once she has prevailed, this state of things, which is evidently a state of unstable equilibrium, must pass away. The age of Constantine must come for Truth sooner or later, though a new Constantine will use new machinery. Truth must sooner or later be in some sense *established*, though by no means in the old sense.

The modern imitation of the primitive Church is unlike its model in this that it does not seriously expect to triumph. It sees the ancient legal churches decline, but it sees their place taken not by the voluntary churches but by secularity or No Church.   Between this and the waning powers of the past the sects or private religions occupy a modest position. They win small triumphs, but no one supposes that the future belongs to them.   Their field of influence seems strictly limited.   They speak of freedom of thought, of the right of private judgment, but they see with anxiety that private judgment is inclined in these days to reject supernaturalism, and without supernaturalism they know no way of distinguishing themselves from schools of "mere philosophy."   The primitive Church defied and vanquished philosophy; its modern imitation retires before it.   It parts with one mystery after another in compliance with the spirit of the age, but parts insensibly at the same time with all character and distinct tendency, as a river broadening towards its mouth ceases to be a river and to have an onward movement just when the banks that confined it fall away on either side.

For us the question is whether, if the present tendency prevails and supernaturalism dies out in established and voluntary churches alike, there will remain the materials out of which a church in the public sense, that is, a great and commanding union of hearts and minds, can be formed. Or must it be admitted that Natural Religion, whatever may be its other advantages, cannot hold a church together?

Let us remark that though those ancient religions which had such a mighty authority rested usually upon the belief in a divine intervention, the intervention was not in quite all cases supernatural. Among the most powerful of those religions has been Mohammedanism, and yet Mohammed professed to perform no miracles. Here then is an example of Natural Religion which nevertheless has been no mere philosophy. And if miracles may be dispensed with we may conceive that even the name of God may be dispensed with, provided the reality which answers to that name is not wanting. That Eternal Law of the Universe which has been treated here as equivalent to God might form the basis of a great religion if only it revealed itself by evidence as convincing to the modern mind as that of miracles was to the mind of antiquity.

When men say "mere philosophy" they mean something arguable, something deniable. Now the case is altered when philosophy changes its name and becomes science. No one says "mere science."

The God in whom the modern world believes has also his Revelation. The solid methods by which truth is separated from mere opinion and science winnowed out of philosophy open a new fountain of prophecy, and give once more a public, authoritative character to truth.

Private judgment is the cry which has been used with success against the ancient churches. It has been declared absurd to expect agreement of opinion in large multitudes of men. Each individual, it is said, thinks as he cannot help thinking, and that will not be as his neighbour thinks —*quot homines tot sententiae.* This principle must no doubt be fatal to churches—as it must be fatal to all co-operation for high purposes among men. If against churches it has been successful, the reason is that as a matter of fact their dogmas had come to seem only questionable opinions and by no means certain truths. Now properly speaking it is not a questionable opinion, but an unquestionable one which a church guards; it is an opinion in which a community lives and which it breathes as its atmosphere, an opinion or way of viewing the Universe which makes the community to be a community and gives it the power to rule itself and make laws for itself. That the dogmas of modern churches are not of this kind is most true, but it is most false that there has never been such an unquestionable opinion, wholly different from mere philosophy, and it is false also that there will never be such an opinion again.

Is it true that the modern world has and can have no such unquestioned universal opinion? The answer will be "Not upon religious or theological questions. On other subjects there may be agreement, more perhaps than in former periods; but upon these questions we see only increasing disagreement or increasing despair. Among active minds there is either individual belief and solitary worship, or else there is a reasoned opinion that no theology is possible and that religion is obsolete." It has been urged here that this current view proceeds upon an utterly loose definition, both of religion and of theology, and that it is only true of particular religions and theologies framed on the received ecclesiastical pattern. It has been urged that a new theology and a new religion have grown up unobserved outside the ecclesiastical sphere. But is this new system a "mere philosophy"? in other words, is it a mere limited influence capable at the utmost only of organising a new sect, or is it one of those great prevalent ways of thinking in which whole generations walk, one of those great atmospheres of thought and feeling which embrace whole lands and continents and furnish the breath of life to vast populations? If it is the latter rather than the former, and if it rests on evidence which though not supernatural has equal cogency to the modern mind, then the new religion is a religion in the old, grand, public sense of the word.

Let us look again for a moment at that old, once universally accepted idea of religion. Surely in recent times we have been misled by exceptional circumstances, by the religious disagreement that has prevailed ever since the Reformation, to form a wrong notion of the very province of religion. That province is much more national and political, much less personal, than is commonly supposed. Religion is not a man's private philosophy, whether that be based on reason or on revelation. It is the atmosphere of common thought and feeling which surrounds a community; because all at once breathe it and live on it, therefore it is a religion. Upon the history of religion this peculiarity is written in characters so large that nothing but the violent drift of modern society in an opposite direction could have made us blind to it. But we are under a prepossession which causes us to overlook the leading part which *nationalities* have played in the great religious revolutions and to attribute everything to persons and individual opinions. We imagine religions to make their way either, like scientific doctrines, through their truth, or else through some adaptation to human needs, and do not perceive that commonly they are what may be called nationalities in an idealised form.

Even in modern Europe we can observe the affinity which exists between the spirit of nationality and that of religion. "Italy," said Mazzini, "is itself a religion." Yes! the view of life, the way of thinking which has become characteristic of a nation, constitutes a sort of atmosphere round the individual members of it, an influence moulding the character of each successive generation which arises to represent it. Any shock or change which makes the individual aware of this atmosphere about him, raises nationality into religion. "By the waters of Babylon" Jewish nationality is transformed into Judaism. Not otherwise at this day the American who finds himself in Europe translates of sheer necessity his American ways of thinking into a creed; he can think and talk of nothing else; to every European he preaches, like St. Paul, "in season and out of season," America, America. And when the shock has been given by some tragic catastrophe, as in the case of ancient Jerusalem or modern Italy, the creed of nationality becomes solemn and intense, so that the suffering patriot says in all seriousness that his country is to him a religion.

This phenomenon so often recurring may almost be called the key to religious history. We should find it in every page of the Bible did we not carefully interpret it away by giving an artificial meaning to all such words as Israel, Zion, Jerusalem. We should see, if we could forget the glosses, that we have before us the long epic of the formation, growth, sufferings, death and resurrection of a nationality. The nationality rises again idealised and diffused in the form of a world-religion. How blind to see in the

triumph of Christianity merely the prevalence of certain
doctrines about the unseen world, merely the work of
persons or the success of a philosophy, and not rather the
idealisation of the Jewish nationality! It is the extension
of the Jewish citizenship to the Gentiles. It is this so truly
that the nations of Europe actually adopt as their own the
entire history and literature of Israel, so that Jewish traditions, heroes and poets supersede everywhere the native
treasure of memory. What more could Mazzini desire for
his Italy than that her Dante and Michael Angelo should be
for the world what the Jews have seen their David and
Isaiah become through Christianity?

Still more completely do we mistake the nature of
another religious revolution only less great than this through
our ignorance of the close connexion between religion and
nationality. The rise of Latin Christianity and of the
Papacy is an event, the grandeur of which is utterly lost
upon those who understand only private religion. They
can see nothing in it but a corruption or perhaps a fraud.
They do not see that the shipwreck of the Western Empire
in the midst of the barbaric invasions was to the Roman
world what the Babylonish captivity was to the Jewish, and
that as the latter event created Judaism the former could not
but call into existence Romanism. They do not see that the
Holy Roman Empire of the Middle Ages is to Rome just
what the Christian Church is to Judaism, that it is the
resurrection of a fallen nationality in an idealised shape.

Look almost where you will in the wide field of history,
you find religion, whenever it works freely and mightily,
either giving birth to and sustaining states, or else raising

them up to a second life after their destruction. It is a great state-builder in the hands of Moses and Ulfilas and Gregory and Nicholas; in the ruder hands of Mohammed and many another tamer and guide of gross populations down to the Prophet of Utah it has the same character, the same too in the hands of the almost forgotten Numas and propagators of the Apollo-worship who laid the foundation of Roman and Greek civilisation, and of the pilgrim fathers who founded New England. In the East to this day nationality and religion are almost convertible terms; the Scotch national character first awoke in the adoption of a new religion and afterwards expressed itself more than once in national covenants; the Reformation itself may be represented as coming out of the German national consciousness, and it has been proposed to call the various forms of Protestantism by the collective name of Teutonic Christianity. Lastly in Christianity itself, in Romanism, and partly also in Mohammedanism, we see religion in the form of an aggressive or missionary nationality bringing foreign nations into a new citizenship.

All this being overlooked, the very outlines of European development disappear from our view. In losing sight of the connexion between religion and nationality we lose the clue to the struggle of Church and State, which is the capital fact in the development of Europe. As in the first part of the struggle we overlook that the Church is but another aspect of the Empire, and Catholicism but the embodiment of the Roman nationality, so in the later stages of it, in the modern struggle between Catholicism and that which calls itself the State, we are blind to the fact that under the so-called State there lurks a new, yet undeveloped Church. For State and Church belong together, and the link between them is nationality. As the Church without the State becomes a mere philosophical or quasi-philosophical sect, so the State without the Church (*i.e.* without a living conscious nationality) is a mere administrative machine, the feeble-ness of which has been brought to light in the revolutions of the nineteenth century. On the other hand, a State animated by a Church acquires a kind of nationality even when nationality in the strictest sense is wanting to it. Thus the Roman world was naturally but a congeries of nations forced together by conquest, but religion made it one, till the phrases *Orbis Romanus* and *Populus Christianus* became convertible terms. And the modern states which boast so loudly of their absolute secularity, or even of their hostility to religion, are not content in practice to be merely secular, as is shown by their eagerness to get the control of education. They study to form out of their own separate nationality a new religion, to revive as far as they can the national religions which gave so vivid a life to the states of antiquity.

If these views are just, if under the modern State there lurks an undeveloped Church and behind the Catholic Church there remain traces of the ancient imperial state, then the prevalent notion of the Church as dying and the secular State as destined soon to prevail against it is not less erroneous than we have found other popular notions about religion to be. The momentary evanescence of the Church in modern life is only caused by the decay of one sort of church coinciding in time with the infancy of another. In the ancient world the Church of single nationalities was vigorous, in the medieval world the Catholic Church of the Roman world-state; in the modern world we see the decline of the latter coinciding with the revival of the former. But if so, what is to be expected? That we shall end where we began, that the last traces of a universal Church will disappear and national religions increase and compete against each other? Surely not. The revival of the separate nationality will be checked after a certain point; never again can the Nation eclipse Humanity; and in the modern world the national spirit, though it refuses to be suppressed, is too narrow and provincial to play the first part. Already we see the necessary reaction against it setting in, and the complaint is heard that it has revived national antipathies and has filled the world with gigantic armies.

We may look then for a counter revival of that cosmopolitan system which was represented in the Middle Ages by the Empire-Church. The universal nationality restored to vigour will once more embrace the local nationalities, the provinces of humanity. Such a universal nationality, like all nationalities, will require both a State and a Church. What then will be the Catholic Church of the future?

The Church, according to the view here taken, is the atmosphere of thought, feeling and belief that surrounds the State; it is, in fact, its civilisation made more or less tangible and visible. What then is the Universal Church but universal civilisation? When a Universal Church stood out in visible shape before men, that is, in the middle ages, what was it but the embodiment of universal civilisation as then understood ?    A universal civilisation exists now not less certainly.    If it is less visibly embodied this is perhaps because it suffers less pressure, because it is not now in constant danger of destruction from Hun and Arab, Turk and Mongol.

We can point to an example of such an unembodied religion which never attained to be regarded as anything more than a form of civilisation.    Among the idealised nationalities enumerated just now one was omitted, in some respects the most influential of all.    Did then the Greek nationality never assume an ideal form?    Assuredly it did. Hellenism is a phenomenon as conspicuous as either Judaism or Romanism.    But Judaism and Romanism are the names of religions, whereas Hellenism was never recognised as a religion but only as a form of civilisation.    Perhaps this was owing to the fact that its diffusion in the world was not accompanied by any tragedy or national agony exciting intense emotions.    In any case it has been an influence not less powerful, enduring, and beneficial than that of most religions, and it has been an influence of essentially the same kind.

It is possible that modern civilisation ought to be content with an influence not more palpably embodied than this. We cannot consider what a mighty force religion has shown itself in creating and sustaining states without recollecting at the same time what terrible things it has done, and perhaps congratulating ourselves that religion in that ancient sense of the word seems now an exhausted volcano.    A sane man cannot wish back again the Church of the middle ages, even though he may recognise all the grandeur and beneficence of it in its place and time. The important thing is not that we should have visible ecclesiastical institutions, but that we should feel ourselves to have our religion, although we call it only civilisation, that the modern world too should be in its way a Jerusalem, an Athens, and no mere secular Babel.

Religion in the individual was identified above with culture; religion in its public aspect now appears to be identical with civilisation. And as culture was shown to be a threefold devotion to Beauty, Goodness, and Truth, it will appear that the term civilisation expresses the same threefold religion, shown on a larger scale in the characters, institutions, and ways of life of nations.

When Western civilisation is confronted with the races outside it or the classes that have sunk below it, what does it feel irresistibly impelled to teach? Science, that is definiteness of conception, accuracy of observation and computation, intellectual conscientiousness and patience, and closely connected with these, the active spirit which rejects fatalism and believes that man's condition can be bettered by his efforts. What else? Humanity, not limited by tribe or nation, and including all principles affecting man's dealings with his kind, respect for women, respect for individual liberty, respect for misfortune. Again what else? Delight and confidence in nature, opposed alike to the superstitious dread of idolatry and to the joylessness of monasticism or puritanism.

This, then, is our civilisation; and what is the religion that inspires it? That scientific spirit of observation and method is the worship of God, whose ways are not as our

ways, but whose law is eternal, and in the knowledge of
whom alone is solid wellbeing   That spirit of active
humanity is Christianity, and it is supplemented by several
other forms of the worship of Man which have grown up
round it.   Lastly, that enjoyment of the visible world is a
fragment saved from the wreck of Paganism.   It is the
worship of the forms of Nature derived from Greece, first
widely diffused at the *Renaissance*, and welcomed since and
spread still more widely by artist natures from age to age.

We have remarked that a civilisation or religion which
to those who live in the midst of it is imperceptible as
an atmosphere becomes distinctly visible in contrast with
the outer world.   Greeks felt their Hellenism in contact
with barbarism and Jews their election in contact with the
Gentiles.   When the contrast becomes intense a condition
of unstable equilibrium is created; the religion becomes
aggressive or missionary, and one of those great spiritual
movements takes place which mark at long intervals the
progress of humanity, such as the conversion of all nations
to Judaism, to Romanism, to Hellenism.   Now there never
was a time when the equilibrium was so unstable as it is now
between the great ruling civilisation of the world, which is
no longer the narrow civilisation of some single city or tribe,
but the great common tradition of a brotherhood of great
nations, and the outlying peoples.   Whereas in past times
the better civilisation had to protect itself from destruction
and became missionary in self-defence, now it is rather
tempted to be apathetic from too triumphant superiority.
It weighs the question whether barbarism should not rather
be exterminated than converted, and while it does so the

question answers itself, for the nations are baptized with gin and the chaff of humanity is burnt up with unquenchable fire-water.

Thus the modern religion finds a vast work ready for its hands, a work which will compel it to give itself some organisation. The children of modern civilisation are called to follow in the footsteps of Paul, of Gregory, of Boniface, of Xavier, Eliot, and Livingstone; but they must carry not merely Christianity in its narrow clerical sense but their whole mass of spiritual treasures to those who want them. Let us carry the true view of the Universe, the true astronomy, the true chemistry, and the true physiology to polytheists still lapped in mythological dreams; let us carry progress and free-will to fatalist nations and to nations cramped by the fetters of primitive custom; let us carry the doctrine of a rational liberty into the heart of Oriental despotisms; in doing all this—not indeed suddenly or fanatically, nor yet pharisaically, as if we ourselves had nothing to learn—we shall admit the outlying world into the great civilised community, into the modern City of God.

A phenomenon so unique as the marriage of England and India ought, if anything can, to give life and distinct shape to the religion of civilisation among us. India wants so much that England has to give, even if we grant that there is much also which we might learn from India. But what precisely have we to give, and in what way precisely ought it to be given? For assuredly we have also much to give that India does *not* want, that would be ruinous to her. We are required therefore rigorously to test our own civilisation, to ask ourselves what influence goes forth from us, how far our spiritual contact is life-giving and how far it may be noxious and noisome. And in thus probing our civilisation we cannot but be led to perceive that it is something wholly different from our mere institutions, that it is a personal influence issuing at the same time out of each individual Englishman, and if we try to define it we shall be led at last to confess that it is neither more nor less than our religion.

But along with it there goes forth from us also our irreligion, and still more, our false religion. And so India gets from England not only the rigorous and commanding science of the West, not only its Christian humanity enlarged by Teutonic liberty, not only its less dreamy enjoyment of life, but also all English heresies, all our deviations from the line of true civilisation, all our ignorances, rudenesses, and shortcomings. The national faults, which we so readily pardon in ourselves, which we smile at and are half proud of, may well frighten us when we see them magnified in the total working of the whole nation upon another nation, and still more in the general impression produced by England upon mankind. Our want of any high ideal, the commonness of our aims and of our lives, the decay of that strong individuality which used to be our boast, our want of any moral greatness which may at all correspond to the wide extension and prosperity of the English race, all this which we fondly misname our common-sense, our honest plainness and practicality, may well frighten us when we view it thus, and may almost fill us with the foreboding of an ignominious national fall.

These and such as these are the thoughts which belong to religion, these far more than speculations about cosmogony or miracles or a future life. Witness the Hebrew prophets themselves, including the last and greatest of them all! Their great topic was always the destiny of cities and nations, the rise and fall of kingdoms, national sins and punishments, and whether "in the judgment it should be more tolerable" for this city or for that.

But if modern civilisation ought to become missionary it ought to embody itself in something of the nature of a church. And thus we arrive at the Church of the Natural Religion.

A church without supernaturalism! The idea is so little familiar to us that it may be well to state distinctly at this point the difference between the conception here presented of a church and that which is current.

For the current notion which is somewhat as follows :—
That an absolutely unique supernatural occurrence, namely, the Resurrection of Jesus, called into existence an absolutely unique institution called the Church ; that the progress of scepticism in modern times having thrown doubt on the reality of this occurrence, the Church is likely to fall, and that after the fall of the Church human society will be left purely secular—we are led to substitute a view which may be thus stated: That every community has in a form more or less organised that for which Christianity furnished a name, that is a church, or rather that every such community is in one aspect a church as in another it is a state ; that Christianity was the instrument by which the universal state, the Roman Empire, completed itself and became also a church ; that

the growth of new states in the bosom of the ancient Empire has created a powerful reaction against the universal religion, because each new state is ambitious of having a religion and a church to itself; that the decline of the ancient Church paves the way not to secularity but to a new growth of national religions such as those of the ancient world; but that the ancient Church has left behind it a conception of universal civilisation, which holds in check these national religions, and out of which a new universal church and religion is likely to grow; so that it seems likely that, as the ancient world had national religions and the medieval world a universal religion, the future will witness national religions flourishing inside a grand universal religion.

It is not solely in order to deal with the outlying populations that the universal religion might well embody itself in a church. There is a domestic problem no less urgent. It is not only for foreign exportation that civilisation needs to be concentrated into a doctrine; without such concentration it can scarcely maintain itself at home. This is no new-fangled notion, but one of the oldest and best authorised observations. All old philosophers knew that the fabric of the State rested ultimately upon a way of thinking, a habit of opinion, a "discipline," which was a thing so delicate and easily deranged that in the opinion of some of them new tunes coming into vogue might be enough to cause a revolution. If this was true then, in a world comparatively quiet, in communities subject to few shocks of thought, how much more true must it be in the vast organisation of later times? That impalpable way of thinking needed afterwards, in the age of migrations, to harden itself into an iron doctrine guarded by a potent priesthood; thus only could the great miracle of human history be accomplished, civilisation and the unity of it be preserved. Another universal danger now threatens. The tide of barbarism might be stemmed by spiritual authority; the tide of thought, scepticism, and discovery which has set in since can be stemmed by no such means. No wise man indeed wishes to stem it; and yet in some way it must be warded off the institutions which it attacks as recklessly as if its own existence did not depend on them. It introduces everywhere a sceptical condition of mind, which it recommends as the only way to real knowledge; and yet if such scepticism became practical, if large communities came to regard every question in politics and law as absolutely open, their institutions would dissolve, and science, among other things, would be buried in the ruin.

Modern thought brings into vogue a speculative Nihilism which explodes traditional theories, such, for instance, as the theory of Monarchy; but unintentionally it creates at the same time a practical Nihilism which explodes and annihilates the Monarch himself!

There is a mine under modern society which, if we consider it, has been the necessary result of the abeyance in recent times of the idea of the Church. There is a total want of correspondence between the views of the people and the system under which they live. The body wants a soul, the State wants a Church. This is equally true of the populations which are still conservative as it is of those which are revolutionary. The link has been broken which united the mass to the advanced minds. The people have long ceased to understand or to follow their own. development.

In England the ideas of the multitude are perilously divergent from those of the thinking class. No sufficient pains have been taken to diffuse everywhere the real religion of the age. Accordingly a large section of the people adhere to the limited religion of the past as it was in the last age of the real efficiency of ecclesiastical organisations, and another large section have abandoned this and have gained no other religion in its place. No adequate doctrine of civilisation is taught among us. Science only penetrates either in the form of useful information or else in that of a negative doctrine opposed to religion; as itself a main part of religion, as the grand revelation of God in these later times supplementing rather than superseding older revelations, it remains almost as much unknown as in the dark ages. Still less known perhaps is that doctrine of the gradual development of human society which alone can explain to us the present state of affairs, give us the clue to history, save us from political aberrations, and point out the direction of progress. So long as churches were efficient this idea of the continuity of civilisation was kept before the general mind. A grand outline of God's dealings with the human race, drawn from the Bible and the church doctrine, a sort of map of history, was possessed by all alike. Are we sufficiently aware what bewilderment must arise when this is no longer the case, when those old outlines grow unserviceable, but no new map is furnished?

Such bewilderment may continue for a long time passive.

In a country like England, a country of publicity and reform, where political institutions do not press overwhelmingly upon the individual, where, for instance, there is no conscription, the absence of any doctrine of civilisation may but make public opinion perplexed and vacillating, so as to cause the nation to seem unworthy of its position in the world. But this same bewilderment, which here produces only dulness, leads on the Continent to revolutionary frenzy. There the old instructress of nations, the Church, has not merely declined in influence but is regarded as a malignant deceiver ; there too the pressure of governments is severely felt. The result is a body without a soul, institutions without corresponding ways of thought, or, in other words, a State without a Church. The suffering individual, instead of seeing in the institutions around him *his* institutions, the house *he* lives in, sees no connexion between himself and them, knows not how they came or why they exist, and suspects them to be but the walls of a prison into which he has been entrapped by a conspiracy of priests and kings. One doctrine of civilisation he has rejected as false, and he conceives no other except the wild improvised conjecture that it has been from the beginning a wicked imposture.

The truth is that religion is and always has been the basis of societies and of states. It is no mere philosophy, but a practical view of life which whole communities live by. For this purpose it must have a basis more solid than mere individual opinion. What can this basis be ? " Divine revelation and miracle," said men in past times. They said so because then miracles had an overwhelming, awe-striking effect beyond ordinary evidence. But a change of opinion

--

has taken place, so that miracles, instead of compelling belief, have now the effect of provoking disbelief.    Is then religion henceforth impossible?

But in proportion as miracles have declined, scientific method has risen, in credit.    Why should it not then be capable by this time of doing what in old times only miracle could do?    " Ah ! but unhappily science refuses its testimony on the very points which are most essential.    We want a future life, a heaven which will atone for all our sufferings here, and science will not give us one."

True, this purpose of religion science will not serve. But it is by no means the only purpose of religion.    From history we learn that the great function of religion has been the founding and sustaining of states.    And at this moment we are threatened with a general dissolution of states from the decay of religion.    Now it does not seem impossible without miracle and using scientific method alone as our organ of discovery to lay down such a Natural Religion as may serve at least this purpose, and may be a sustaining principle to the civilisation of the world.

# CHAPTER V

## NATURAL RELIGION AND THE CHURCH

WE have been led on from the conception of a Natural Religion to that of a Natural Church. We have not thought of it as a mere utopia, which may or may not sooner or later be realised. This Church exists already, a vast communion of all who are inspired by the culture and civilisation of the age. But it is unconscious, and perhaps if it could attain to consciousness it might organise itself more deliberately and effectively.

Now there exists by the side of this a Church which has had from ancient times consciousness and organisation. It is still vigorous and influential, especially in this country, Ought the vast unconscious Church here described to disregard the conscious Church, and ought it to organise itself independently? Or should it regard the existing Church organisation as rightfully its own, and as capable by reform of being adapted to its purposes? For thus when fifty years ago a new England had sprung up in vast manufacturing towns of which Parliament knew nothing, that new England did not frame for itself a new Parliament, but called for a Reform Bill which admitted it into the old.

The hindrance to such a course is obvious enough, and yet it must seem strange to those who arrive at the notion of a church as we have done. The great ideas which lie at the basis of civilisation do indeed demand much study from those who are to teach them, but we are not disturbed by the fear that of able and serious men undertaking such study, a large proportion will end by rejecting the ideas as untrue. Or if such a doubt should arise we should think it ought to be met by reconsidering, and, if necessary, altering the accepted doctrine. We should certainly not think it ought to be met by rigidly excluding all such heterodox candidates, however numerous, however able, however serious. The clergy of such a church as has been here described, if it should have a clergy, would be subjected to no tests of opinion, but only to tests of character and competence. It would be held that liberty of opinion was the first condition of their efficiency as teachers.

Now this, which is stated here as self-evident, is almost universally considered monstrous and almost a contradiction in terms. Freethinking is understood to be the opposite of religion, and accordingly membership in a church is supposed to imply a restriction upon the liberty of thought. The very idea of freethinking as an important condition of religion, and especially of efficient religious teaching, provokes ridicule ; it has been described as "a medley of St. Paul and St. Voltaire." But if we have succeeded in drawing the distinction between religion and philosophy, it will now be clear that a church is wholly unlike a philosophical school, held together by doctrines. If, as we have held, it is more like a state than a school, doctrinal tests will begin to seem more absurd than the absence of them. Imagine a state resting upon dogma !

Suppose we had formulated in the sixteenth century the principles or beliefs which we supposed to lie at the basis of our national constitution. Suppose we had made a political creed. Perhaps the doctrine of divine right and the power of kings to cure disease, perhaps the whole legend of Brute and the derivation of our state from Troy would have appeared in this creed. Once formulated, it would have come to be regarded as the dogmatic basis upon which our society rested. Then in time criticism would have begun its work. Philosophy would have set aside divine right, science would have exploded the belief about the king's evil, historical criticism would have shaken the traditionary history, and each innovation would have been regarded as a blow dealt at the constitution of the country. At last it would have come to be generally thought that the constitution was undermined, that it had been found unable to bear the light of modern science. Men would begin publicly to renounce it ; officials would win great applause by resigning their posts from conscientious doubts about the personality of King Arthur ; and those who continued orthodox would declare that they felt more respect for such persons, much as they deplored their heresies, than they could feel for other officials who continued to receive the emoluments of the State when it was suspected that they had altogether ceased to believe in the cure of the king's evil, and when they explained away with the most shameless laxity the divine right of the sovereign. If any of this latter school, whom we may call the Broad State, should argue

that the State was a practical institution, not a sect of people
united by holding the same opinions, that it existed to save
the country from invasion and houses from burglary, they
would be regarded as impudent sophists.  "Was not the
creed there?   Were not all officials required to subscribe it?
How then could it be affirmed that the State did not stand
upon community of opinion, upon dogma?"   And if any
of these sophists were evidently not impudent, but well-
meaning and high-minded, they would be regarded as
wanting in masculine firmness and the courage to face
disagreeable truths.   It would be generally agreed that the
honest and manly course was to press the controversy firmly
to a conclusion, to resist all attempts to confuse the issue,
and to keep the public steadily to the fundamental points.
Has the sovereign, or has he not, a divine right?   Can he,
or can he not, cure disease by his touch?   Was the country,
or was it not, colonised by fugitives from Troy?   And if at
last the public should come by general consent to decide
these questions in the negative, then it would be felt that
no weak sentiment ought to be listened to, no idle gratitude
to the constitution for having, perhaps, in past times saved
the country from Spanish or French invasion ; that all such
considerations ought sternly to be put aside as irrelevant ;
that as honest men we were bound to consider, not whether
our constitution was useful or interesting, or the like, but
whether it was *true*, and if we could not any longer say with
our hands on our hearts that it was so, then, in the name of
eternal truth, to renounce it and bid it farewell!

Now why should churches, if they are not mere philosophical schools, be bound by dogma more than states?

Institutions are not mere machines; they are also organisms; they have a certain power of gradual self-modification analogous to growth. And they have this power usually in proportion to their healthy vigour. Thus it is that the English State has weathered the storms of a thousand years. If now it is a thing profoundly different from the England over which Edward the Confessor ruled, the change has been made in the same insensible manner by which the child with its tender limbs, vague, dreamy thoughts and fickle instinctive motions, passes into the man with his strong-set frame, fixed habits, and sure logical trains of reflection. And that it has been capable of such a gradual transformation is the best evidence of the healthy vitality which has animated it. There could have been no more certain proof that it was but half alive or that the English nation, like some other nations, wanted the political sense necessary for forming a state worthy of the name, than an inability to pass through such modifications silently, or a disposition, whenever such changes became necessary, to dissolve the State on the ground that it no longer answered its original definition, perhaps with some vague intention of afterwards forming a new one.

Such a rigid definition are the formularies and articles by which churches bind themselves. A church cannot any more than a state submit to such trammels without confessing that it is not really alive, and that it is a machine rather than a living organism.

Nor has a church any strong hold on life if it only deems itself in a healthy condition while it continues to be what it was originally, or if it thinks to cure its ailments by undoing all the modifications which time has brought and restoring its original shape.   This process is called in the Church reformation and is thought of as an evidence of vigour; and of this kind are almost all movements which go on within the Church, that is, they are returns upon the past, revivals of what was dead, reinstitution of what was obsolete.

Such anxious retrospectiveness would not be thought a healthy symptom in other institutions.   Life looks onward, not backward; the man does not pride himself upon being precisely like the boy, but there does come a time when he regrets to perceive himself altered, and we know what this means; it means that he has begun to decay.

An institution is healthy in proportion to its independence of its own past, to the confident freedom with which it alters itself to meet new conditions.

In this volume an attempt has been made to treat the subject of religion in a practical manner.   We have asked the question, Is there really such a thing as religion in the sense in which our fathers took the word, that is, not some faint feeling in feminine minds, not some hardly discernible subtlety of a special school of philosophers, but a thing obvious, palpable, huge, filling the earth and the sky and dwarfing everything else by its magnitude?   Of course this can only be, and yet people not know it, if some egregious mistake of nomenclature has been made, so that what past generations used to call religion has now got another name or names, and the word religion has been transferred to some-thing of less importance.   This then has been asserted.   It has been shown that the multitude, fixing their eyes, as is their wont, only upon the outsides of things, have identified religion with its organisation, with churches and chapels, with the clerical profession and its interests. They have accordingly mistaken the fact that this organisation has ceased to be efficient for a decline in religion itself. But it has seemed to us that though religion runs shallow or scarcely runs at all in its old channel, this is only because the stream has been drawn off in other directions. We have found the substance of religion still existing, but outside its old organisation, broken up and distributed under other names or under no name. Man has still grand spiritual interests, which are all-important to him and which he partly feels to be so; only to his misfortune he has ceased to think of them together in the whole which they constitute. If he could view them thus they would affect him with the same solemn anxiety which we trace in ancient utterances concerning religion. He would see that religion is everything, if not precisely in the sense of those who talk of an endless heaven or hell awaiting each individual, yet in the sense of the ancient prophets who watched over the weal of their Jerusalem. He would see that on religion depends the whole fabric of civilisation, all the future of mankind.

Now the clear recognition of this in churches would make it possible for them to live again with a healthy life. All that retrospectiveness, that unhealthy inclination for revival and what is called reformation, proceeds from a conscious perplexity about the object for which churches exist. Those who cannot see the end fix their eyes, as the next best thing, upon the beginning, as in politics also fantastic revivals are sometimes undertaken by immature or dilettante

P

politicians. All such aberrations spring from want of serious-ness, and seriousness consists in knowing what you desire, in consciously willing the end and willing the means. If in churches there were found the seriousness that is found in states, if the spiritual interests were as vividly clear to the churchman as those partly material, partly spiritual interests which occupy the politician are clear to him, we should see the same free and inventive adaptation of means to ends in ecclesiastical as in secular politics.

An attempt has here been made to consider the Church with reference rather to its end than to its beginning. It has been shown that religion does not always need any very palpable embodiment, but that in very large communities there is danger lest for want of a doctrine of civilisation, and therefore an organised Church, multitudes should grow up without any acquaintance or sympathy with the order in which they live. Now of all such great social organisms the largest ever seen on earth is that to which we ourselves belong, the great whole of which the Christian Church once formed the soul and the European system, an Empire slowly dissolving into a brotherhood of States, was the body. Being so large and having institutions so complicated, it does need much spiritual machinery. And yet in the last century or so this machinery has been wanting, owing chiefly to the self-assertion of the smaller national organisms which conceal partial national religions. The result has been what might have been expected, a result of which few yet measure the awful importance. It is something which almost threatens the death of the organism, that is, of European civilisation itself. It is a vast rebellion of the less prosperous classes against the whole system which has nursed them, a fierce repudiation on their part of the whole system or law, way of viewing the Universe or worship, which lies at the basis of the civilised world. It includes a mortal hatred against all visible authority, a complete political revolution.

This movement is not to be confounded with the movement of reform. The reformers are those who desire to advance civilisation, which they regard as a gradual development. They are therefore adverse to everything like immobility, and even believe that change ought now to advance with some degree of rapidity. Naturally therefore their attack upon survivals and abuses is often vehement and bitter. But it is echoed in quite another tone by a vast host who are so far from holding this doctrine of development that they are quite unable to conceive it. These are not reformers or progressists. Their conceptions are of the archaic primitive kind. They hold that happiness is a fixed thing within easy reach of all, and that civilisation is the mass of frauds by which it is appropriated to the few. Their object therefore is not to advance civilisation, but to destroy it by assassination and massacre.

If we really believe that a case can be made out for civilisation, this case must be presented by popular teachers, and their most indispensable qualification will be independence. They perhaps will be able to show that happiness, or even universal comfort, is not, and never has been, within quite so easy reach, that it cannot be taken by storm, and that as for the institutions left us from the past they are no more diabolical than they are divine, being the fruit of necessary development far more than of freewill or calcula-

tion. Such teachers would be the free clergy of modern
civilisation. It would be their business to investigate and
to teach the true relation of man to the Universe and to
society, the true Ideal he should worship, the true vocation
of particular nations, the course which the history of mankind has taken hitherto, in order that upon a full view of
what is possible and desirable men may live and organise
themselves for the future. In short, the modern Church is
to do what Hebrew prophecy did in its fashion for the Jews,
and what bishops and Popes did according to their lights for
the Roman world when it laboured in the tempest, and for
barbaric tribes first submitting themselves to be taught.

Another grand object of the modern Church would be
to teach and organise the outlying world, which for the
first time in history now lies prostrate at the feet of Christian civilisation.

Here are the ends to be gained. These once recognised,
the means are to be determined by their fitness alone. The
question is not what means the Church employed in other
times, for other times had other problems, not what was
done by Paul or Gregory or Luther, but what men who,
like Paul, Gregory, and Luther, knew what they were about,
would be likely to do now.

But if so, why should we delay while we puzzle ourselves
with the question, "Are we really members of the Church
or not? Can we conscientiously call ourselves Christian?
Is the Christian religion true? Is it not necessary, before
we can act, to invent a new religion?" The *truth* of a
religion is a phrase without meaning. You may speak of
the truth of a philosophy, of a theory, of a proposition, but

not of a religion, which is a condition of the feelings. Nor ought we to speak about joining or leaving a church as if a church were a philosophic school or a political party. A church is the social organism into which a man is born ; his membership in it, like his membership in a state, is not a matter of opinion or belief, nor is it to be put on or off at pleasure. And as to the Christian Church, it is simply the spiritual side of the great organism of civilised society throughout the Western world.

The most cross-grained sceptic, the spirit most in love with negation, can scarcely deny the grandeur of the original conception of a universal Church. As we can still trace to some extent the gradual growth of it in the mind of its Founder, it is the largest and highest of all conceptions. That there is something under the State which is not quite the State, a thing as yet unnamed,—shall we call it king-dom of God? shall we call it ecclesia?—and then that, as God is one and Man is one, this something must underlie not each nation only but all mankind taken together—the vision of the whole race passing out of its state of clannish division, as the children of Israel themselves had done in the time of Moses, and becoming fit to receive a universal constitution, this is great. Great too is the temporary realisation of the vision, when the world-church, thus largely sketched, met with a world-state strangely fit to be its com-plement, and so for the first and only time in history Universal Civilisation took visible shape. The thought of human Society as resting on a double basis, of civilised men as the children of a transcendent marriage between the spiritual and the temporal, suggested the image of the

Mother Church, the Wife of the crowned Humanity. At other times a spiritual city was spoken of, which descended from heaven and was set up in the midst of the cities and kingdoms of the earth.

This conception of a spiritual city is precisely what is now needed. But can we recognise the faintest attempt to realise it in the actual organised Church? Does this institution even pretend to perform such a function, to act as the organ of civilisation, as the interpreter of human society? Does it explain to us the development by which we have been brought to our present stage? Does it open to us the vista of the future? Does it make us at home in human history, and so save us from the bewilderment and horror which the past excites when we open its records at random, by showing us how rigorously human progress has always been conditioned, how much is impossible, and at the same time how much and what the laws of history justify us in hoping for? Such guidance was never more needed than now, when this horror is seizing innumerable minds and exciting them to frenzy. But does the Church even pretend to offer it?

We know that for the most part it is occupied with quite other topics. To most of its utterances the active world listens in half-contemptuous silence, feeling that it is useless to controvert the propositions laid down, and that no results would follow from admitting them. The propositions are *archaic;* they show that the Church *once* understood its function and discharged it efficiently. Something evidently has arrested development. What? The retrospectiveness, the anxious fear of ceasing to be what it originally was, which seizes an institution when it has begun to be uncertain why it exists.

But why should the outside public approve such devotion to archaic dogmas, as if it were the only honest and rational course which the Church could take?

Circumstances have created a sort of fixed idea in the public mind, an inveterate association between the belief in certain dogmas and the membership of a certain church. Accordingly a view like that which has been here presented is certain to be met in general with objections like the following :—

" Possibly such a way of regarding religion and the Church may be in itself sound. But in that case the proper inference is that we want a new religion, that we ought to dissolve the present Church and to found another. And perhaps it may be true that 'the good Lord Jesus has had His day,' that other hopes and other beliefs animate the modern world, which when the time is ripe will find their proper embodiment. In that case it is a mark of weakness and vagueness of view to attempt to slur over radical difficulties and to confuse together under a cloudy statement inconsistent ideas. Let us say, if you will, religion will endure, but let us say with firmness, Christianity will die. There may be a church in the future, but it will not be the Christian Church."

The assumption involved in this, viz. that the Christian Church is a society founded upon a dogma, is neither altogether absurd nor quite without plausibility. Such societies there are. Those who have some common conviction and wish to propagate it, adherents of some doctrine or disciples of some master, commonly have some association among themselves, though they seldom go the length of excluding from it all who cannot subscribe a symbol. And if we look, as Protestants are disposed to do, at the original institution of Christianity, we find it growing out of the single alleged fact of the Resurrection, we find St. Paul himself declaring that without that fact it was nothing—the fact being precisely one of those which the modern scientific school puts on one side. On the other hand, the Catholic view is still more pitilessly dogmatic. Here no doubt is explanation enough of the opinion now commonly held about Christianity, and of the tenacity of it.

But a great organic growth such as Christianity, filling so vast an extent both in space and time, is not to be judged by the estimate of any single observer, were it St. Paul himself. The strongest creations of human sociability are not those which have sprung up in the most logical and consciously reasonable way, but rather those which have their roots buried deep in the unconscious part of human nature. Could we penetrate to the origin of Athens, we should not find that conscious artists and conscious philosophers assembled to lay the first stone of it. We should find a simple village-community and one or two temples with a sacred legend preserved in each; scarcely a presentiment of what was to spring from such a germ; only a vague belief to the effect *hunc frondoso vertice collem, quis deus incertum est, habitat deus.* And yet we do not say that the later developments of Athens were illegitimate, abusive; when we read of Solon's impatience at the first modest beginnings of Athenian tragedy we judge him mistaken; we judge that while he thought himself a wise reformer calling the citizens back to first principles he was in reality short-sighted, and that his example proves that the instinct of development in a truly living institution is wiser than the wisest individual man.

It is not very bold to claim for the Christian Church that it has as much right to develop and expand as any political institution that hopes to live must needs have. If at first it sprang out of a local miracle and may have been little distinguished from other waves of feeling that were propagated by the religious guilds of the ancient world, Christianity is not now identical with belief in the Resurrection of Jesus. It is now and has for fifteen centuries been something wholly different, namely, the great bond holding the European races and their offshoots together in that sort of union out of which naturally springs a common polity. True it may be that the miracle was the essential fact without which the union would never have been accomplished ; there may have been a time when it was true that "if Christ be not risen our faith is vain"; but when the union has taken place, has endured for a thousand years, and though since weakened and endangered, yet subsists in the form of an indestructible common civilisation and sense of unity among nations, it is true no longer. The Christian Church is now the visible expression of a true cosmopolitanism which will be eternal, and this being so, it avails nothing henceforth against it to argue that after all Christ is not risen. Nay, no conceivable historic scepticism ought to have the power to shake it, any more than the fabric of imperial Rome at its height would have been shaken if a Beaufort or a Niebuhr had arisen at the court of Augustus to question the personality of Romulus.

Rome was strong because it looked to its end, the Christian Church is now weak because it looks back to its beginning. And here is the difference between the great social fabrics which last for thousands of years and the temporary associations, such as philosophic or political parties, which live only the wearing out of a fashion of thought. So long as an institution has a visible and palpable use, so long as we want and feel that we cannot do without the support of it, so long its continuance cannot be made a question and it has a robust life that no criticism can touch. Thus to most of us the English State seems to exist as necessarily as the sun and moon, and an Englishman does not ask himself anxiously what discoveries historical research is making about our early kings, or whether he *agrees* with Hengist and Horsa.

The Christian Church was once an institution of this kind, of all institutions on the earth incomparably the greatest and firmest ; it was not so much like the sun in the heaven as it was a light of which the sun was a pale reflection. In those ages of slow intellectual movement when all Hellenism, all philosophy or science, was in abeyance for several centuries, it was possible to hold this commanding position for a long time without submitting to much internal modification ; but since man began again to think, to know, and to discover, it has become more evident with every century that churches like states can only live on the condition of changing freely and perpetually. The time has evidently come at last when this must absolutely be admitted, unless the Church would be a martyr to its own dogmas and would lay down a principle which Jesus Christ denied, the principle, namely, of finality in Divine Revelation.

But it may be urged that if this time has come it has come too late for Christianity. " The decline of the Church has advanced so far that there can be no more question of reforming it, even if such a Reformation was still possible two or three centuries ago. A certain amount of corruption might be purged away, languor or debility might be removed by opening new sources of life, but the season of such remedial measures is past. When reformers everywhere find the Church the great obstacle in their path, when it seems the great asylum for all abuses, where they find shelter and an air of sacredness is thrown over them, the time is come for a revolutionary outbreak. *Il faut en finir.* Like Savonarola or Luther or Knox, nay, like Jesus Christ Himself, we must declare war against a hypocritical organisation."

It is not quite extravagant to take this tone against Catholicism. A system which has been associated in the past with so much crime and has so firmly resisted reform provokes this style of opposition, and all the more so because in its abasement it has retained so much grandeur. But neither Jesus Christ, nor Luther and Knox, when they proclaimed the downfall of a corrupt hierarchy, thought of establishing society, by way of reform, upon a secular basis. All alike treated the system they attacked as the perversion of something good and sacred, all alike substituted another church for that which they destroyed. Our modern reformers who wish to hand over what they take from the Church to the State are of a different type. They are of those who do

not understand that there must always be a church, organised
or not, where there is a human society. These are like
children, who confound air, the most necessary of realities,
with vacuum or nothing at all.

But there are some among them who say that no doubt
a new religion and church must be introduced in the room
of Christianity, that it must be a system founded upon
science and embodying the real honest beliefs of the present
age. That such a system ought to be introduced has been
assumed throughout this book ; but is it so evident as not
to be worth discussion that because such a system might in
many important points be inconsistent with the Christianity
of the creeds, therefore it must be introduced as a rival
system, and that a place must be cleared for it by the
destruction of Christianity? Must there needs, so to speak,
be two Acts of Parliament, the first abrogating Christianity
and the second instituting the new system in its place?
Is this the way in which great changes are usually or wisely
·made in the world? Is it not rather evident that the most
extreme opponent of the Christian creed, unless he is a
Secularist, ought to design the reform and not the destruction of the Christian Church?

It may be true that on the Continent reformers are
provoked by the immobility of the Church to take a
revolutionary course, in spite of all the untold evils, the
incurable ulcer of social discord, that may spring from such
a policy. But when we contemplate the religious question
from the Teutonic or Anglo-Saxon point of view we can see
no reason to do so. The Church here looks more like an
organism and less like a vast machine. We can imagine

without much difficulty English and American Christianity taking a shape adapted to the age. We should have little difficulty in conceiving that fixed exclusive dogmas are no more necessary in the Church than in a state or a university or in a philanthropic society; only we are for the time puzzled to give a precise answer to the question, If the Church is not a society holding certain dogmas, what is it?

To this question then we answer as follows : The Church is neither more nor less than the spiritual city of Western civilisation; but this city has been dilapidated by schisms and revolutions so that it is scarcely traceable in the present and is best understood by looking back to the world-church of the middle ages and to the small state-churches of Israel and of Greece. As to dogmas, we say that the word is unsatisfactory, but that the Church so understood does indeed hold certain dogmas in the sense of cherishing certain views of the Universe, certain maxims of life, certain habits and tastes; that, however, it does not pride itself either upon the peculiarity or upon the unchangeableness of these dogmas; that many of them are simple and indisputable enough, mere truisms if considered philosophically, and only made important by being acted upon; that others again it shares with many other religions; that others have been called in question by modern science, with respect to which it only asks that science be not too hasty and do not indulge malice against a rival system, while it professes to be actuated by nothing but a love of truth ; and that others again, the growth of later centuries, have never been formulated into dogmas at all nor recognised by the ecclesiastical authorities, and yet are of priceless value; finally, that a reform is evidently needed by which new truth, such as wells forth so abundantly in the modern world, shall be taken up into the teaching of the Church.

As to the controversy between orthodoxy and science this volume is not concerned with it. True religion, as it is here defined, can never have any conflict with science except when science disregards the claims of humanity. Only as we have a duty to truth, we consider also the interests of the human republic. We reflect that a reckless devotion to the pursuit of truth may endanger the foundations of society partly by shaking too suddenly the beliefs upon which it is founded, partly by creating a dangerous chasm between the philosophic class and the vulgar. We hold therefore that while the dispute between orthodoxy and science continues undecided there should take place a great coalition of all who are serious on both sides. While Science says, " Before we can seriously benefit mankind we must exterminate Christianity," it breaks the continuity of history, sets men at wild war with their own past, alienates all those who by training and disposition feel most tenderly towards mankind, and surrounds itself exclusively with those whose studies are cold, and in some cases foster a ruthless fanaticism. While Christianity devotes itself to a crusade against modern thought, it is likely either to be beaten, if it fights the philosophers with their own weapons, or to rouse the superstitions of the vulgar, if it appeals to feeling against thought. It remains then to make the most of the common ground between them ; this common ground is Natural Religion, and the Christian

Church so far as the Christian Church shows itself to be modifiable.

That Natural Religion is a far larger and more substantial thing than is commonly supposed, that it is indeed as wide as modern civilisation, has been argued at length. On the other hand, why should not the Christian Church open itself to the modifications which the age requires? Any one who should study the nature of Christianity only in the Bible would praise it most of all for this, that more than any other religion it takes account of the claims of time. In the long religious development recorded there nothing is so impressive as the historic piety which binds the successive revelations together. The prophets reverence the lawgiver; Christ and His apostles reverence both; and yet each new revelation asserts its own superiority to those which went before, the superiority not of one thing to another thing but of the developed thing to the undeveloped. It is thus that the ages should behave to one another. Has Christianity lost this secret, this understanding and concert with time? It possessed it assuredly in its first period. The apostolic writings, like the prophetic, are full of the future; they do not look upon all development as ended, but study intently to divine what time will bring next, what new dispensation, what second coming is in store for the Church. But in passing into other races Christianity could not but suffer by being dissociated from the tradition of Jewish prophecy. It could not but lose the prophetic spirit, the eager study of the future.

We have spoken of science as replacing miracle; prophecy it does not so much replace as restore. As it grasps human affairs with more confidence it begins to unravel the past and with the past the future. It shows the significance of each new social or political phase as the Hebrew prophets studied to do. History and prophecy belong together. As it was prophecy that made the old Church modifiable by preparing it to understand each new time, the modern Church may recover the power of development by calling history to its aid. That view of history as a whole which past generations had, when they spoke of the creation of the human race six thousand years ago, of Adam's fall, etc., may seem to us crude, but some such general view we must have if mankind is to be saved from bewilderment and anarchy, an anarchy which is already almost upon us. Such a view grows every year fuller and more distinct through the labours of scientific historians, a view of the past from which the future in some of its large outlines may be inferred. And thus as science replaces the cosmogonies of old religion, history scientifically treated restores the ancient gift of prophecy, and with it may restore that ancient skill by which a new doctrine was furnished to each new period and the old doctrine could be superannuated without disrespect.

Lastly, it is a capital circumstance that the organisation is there, an organisation for working on all mankind at once, which once destroyed could not without vast trouble be replaced. To send a new life through this organisation, the life of science and history, would be a shorter and a cheaper course than to destroy it. But this course would call for a great moral effort. Ecclesiastics would need courage, and the opposite school forbearance. Both alike would need—

and this perhaps in practice would be the hardest require-
ment—to rise above the petty love of petty triumphs, the
degenerate propensity to idle quarrelling; they would need,
in short, the seriousness which comes from the sense that
great issues are at stake, scarcely less indeed than the whole
future of civilisation.

# CHAPTER VI

IT remains to collect together and exhibit in one view the principles to which we have been led separately and successively in the course of this volume.

There is a Lower Life, of which the animating principle is secularity, or—in the popular sense of the word—materialism. This Lower Life is made up of purely personal cares, and pursues even in the midst of civilisation no other object than those which the savage pursues under simpler conditions, self-preservation, personal possession and enjoyment, personal pleasure. The principle of secularity would lead in fact to savage isolation but for the influences which check and thwart it in civilised society, compelling it to wear a disguise and reducing it to a dangerous tendency. The Good Cause of the world consists in resistance to this tendency and detection of its disguises, wherever it is found working not openly in nihilistic outbreaks but insidiously by weakening or perverting the great institutions of co-operative life.

There is a Higher Life, of which the animating principle has been called at different times by different names, but the most comprehensive name for it is religion. It is the influence which draws men's thoughts away from their personal interests, making them intensely aware of other existences, to which it binds them by strong ties sometimes of admiration, sometimes of awe, sometimes of duty, sometimes of love. Under this influence the individual ceases to be a mere individual and becomes the member of some corporate body, whether city or nation or tribe or church, and his acts in consequence begin to have a moral character, as being determined by some motive larger than personal interest. When the influence has operated for a long time upon a whole community, each member of it finds himself amply overpaid for his sacrifices by a richer consciousness, a capacity for more various and finer enjoyment ; the savage becomes a citizen ; and in the midst of the community there grows up a great treasure of institutions, arts, inventions, traditions, refinements, and habits, which is called collectively its civilisation.

But this process suffers interruption and frustration in many ways, principally in two. In the first place the influence which draws together and conglobes certain individuals into a living society acts as intensely in producing discord outside the society as in creating union within it. The corporate bodies, each of which is a nucleus of civilisation, are all at war with each other. The sacrificing Aryan, the " twice-born man," regards all that are outside his sacred community as " devils," against whom he must wage perpetual war ; the Israelite, made suddenly into a hero by his divine law, rushes down upon Hittite and Jebusite, asserting a divine right to their territory ; the Islamite overthrows kingdom after kingdom for no other reason than that his prophet has given him a new principle of life. And by such wars religion often destroys itself. For conquest mixes again the atoms of humanity; it neutralises the religions that held them together, and so disperses them again through doubt and bewilderment. The Romans had not long begun to conquer before they perceived that conquest would destroy the heroism that had made it possible by introducing foreign disciplines. Their foreboding was fulfilled; the Empire of Rome was undermined by moral decay until a new discipline grew up which embraced the whole of it.

This experience of the discords produced by all partial religions, with the example given in the Roman Empire of the way in which such discords may be healed, has put before the minds of men an unfading vision of a universal religion which may unite all mankind at once as the partial religions have united particular communities.

But religions do not only hurt each other by collision, they also decay inwardly. Springing up ordinarily in the infancy of the human mind, they are alloyed from the beginning with mistake and misconception. They are indeed alloyed with something far worse, of which in this volume intentionally nothing has been said, but which it may be well once for all to take note of.

Let it be remarked then that religion has been treated of here only so far as it is a good thing. In comparing religions in order to discover their common property it has always been tacitly assumed that there is a species of religion which is noble, and that our concern was with this alone. But assuredly there is also a species of religion which is bad intrinsically and yet is of such common occurrence that it might almost lay claim to determine the sense which should be given to the word religion. Religion has been regarded here as the link of feeling which attaches man habitually to something outside himself, and it has been assumed that this feeling is always of the nature of admiration and love. But as a matter of fact it is quite as often of the nature of terror. If we chose to describe religion as a nightmare eternally troubling man's repose, depressing all his powers with slavish dread and tempting him to terrible crimes under the name of expiations, history no doubt would amply bear us out. But on the whole in the modern world the better aspect of religion has vindicated itself. The word is now more naturally used in a good sense. It is no longer convertible with superstition. We recognise that men have at times a vision of something mighty and horror-striking which makes them grovel in the dust, and that this is superstition, but that they have also at other times a vision of something as glorious as it is mighty, and that this is religion.

Nevertheless, though we can thus distinguish in thought religion from superstition, we cannot always prevent them from being intricately mixed together in fact. It has rarely been found possible to extract from religion the nobler element, so as to escape suffering at the same time from its wasting influence. Not only in Tauris or in Mexico but here in England religion has been and is a nightmare, and those who flatter themselves that they have shaken off the horror find a colder, more petrifying incubus, that of Annihilation, settling down upon them in its place, so that one of them cries out, *Oh ! reprends ce Rien, gouffre, et rends-nous Satan.*

But even the nobler kind of religion, as it springs up naturally, is full of mistake and misconception.  It finds the man at a certain stage of enlightenment, it lightens up with love and wonder his view of the Universe, but it does not of itself correct that view.  And as religion is one of man's earliest friends, it finds him commonly when his view of the world is not merely a little wrong but childish and fantastic in the extreme.  Out of conceptions half-childish half-poetic it constructs objects of worship, and in the temples built to these and in the sacred poetry and history which grow out of the worship of these, all the poetic childishness is consecrated and perpetuated.  In this way religion, at first the inspiring guide of man, becomes at a later time his tyrant. She who taught him his rudiments opposes his higher education, and with all the more effect that she does it "*with no unworthy aim and e'en with something of a mother's mind.*"

Almost always when religion comes before us historically it is seen consecrating in this manner conceptions obsolete or obsolescent.  The stage in which it fully satisfies the best intellects lasts commonly but a moment.  Then begins a time in which it wants a little help from interpretation. What was meant literally must now be taken figuratively; what was advanced as fact must be received as allegory. Yet still for a long time the very greatest minds range themselves sincerely on the side of belief.  Sceptics may perhaps have witnessed the first representations of Aeschylus, and assuredly there was scepticism in the age of Dante, but Aeschylus and Dante were greater than the sceptics.  How long this period of substantial effective predominance will last depends very much upon the character of the reigning

religion.  It could not last very long in Greece, where the
religion was too evidently primitive and childish though so
lovely.  Italian religion fell speedily into contempt.  But
Christian orthodoxy, to the composition of which so many
and various elements had gone, which was developed in the
midst of advanced politics and advanced philosophy, which
had a broad strong basis in Jewish history and prophecy
and a superstructure composed of materials drawn from
Plato and Aristotle—this was able to hold its own with
ease for many centuries.  When the spirit of inquiry was
reawakened in the twelfth century, the Church was able to
make it subservient and to create a philosophy of her own.
As Dante was orthodox in the fourteenth century, Michael
Angelo was orthodox in the sixteenth.  If Rabelais and
Montaigne knew themselves not to be Christians, if probably
Shakespeare's mind in its immense wanderings had become
acquainted with doubt, yet still throughout the seventeenth
century great and subtle intellects, such as Pascal and
Milton, could feel their spiritual life to be rooted in the
Christian tradition.

A third stage begins in the history of religions when the
best minds begin consciously to admit that their view of the
Universe has altered since the religion was first promulgated.
Then, and not till then, arises a great practical question,
What is to be done?

A question difficult enough in itself; but we complicate
it unnecessarily.  It is an effect of the greatness and
sovereign nature of religion that the particular variety of it
under which we live seems to us the only possible religion.
When therefore this is attacked we do not say, A religion is

in danger! but, Religion is in danger! And the new views
of the Universe are never thought of as a new religion or as
a modification of religion, but as something secular in their
nature.    At best they are called philosophy or science.

And yet what are these philosophies but the freshest
attempts to grasp the Universe? Now are not the religions
which they attack but older attempts to do the same? The
only peculiarity of religion is that it is a philosophy which
has in some past time shaped a community, and therefore
by a kind of necessity, lest the community should fall to
pieces again, holds a sort of monopoly in it. If we make
the extreme supposition, namely, that the reigning religion
is wholly opposed to the new views and must be rejected
wholly, it would still not be immediately certain that religion
as such must suffer or secularity gain, for the new philosophy
might prove a more edifying and ennobling religion than
that which it replaced.

Another unnecessary difficulty which we introduce is to
regard the new system as much more flatly opposed to the
old one than it really is.    Here again religion suffers from
the fact that it has its roots in the primitive period of
society.    For hence it gathers precedents of a rude barbarous
mode of conducting controversy.    In minds accustomed to
philosophic thought a change of opinion does not come by
abrupt cataclysm but by gradual development.    If it be
accompanied by debate, the debate is conducted with
candour and temper.    But religion by its nature is the
ancient philosophy of a whole community, that is, it is a
philosophy of unphilosophical people.    It is discussed therefore, like politics, with wild party spirit and with an eager

desire to make all differences as sharp as possible. Like politics, it is seized as a pretext for fighting, since fighting in one form or another is the salt of life to the majority in most communities. But religious controversy is always some degrees more barbarous than political, as it appeals to more primitive precedents. It imbibes the spirit of an age when war was the business of life, when rude warriors turned dogmas into war-cries. And even to the present day, though we have grown so familiar with the nicety of philosophic distinctions and the delicate handling they require, yet when the subject is theology we grow indignant at anything that looks like compromise, think the edge of controversy cannot be too sharp, and insensibly take crusaders and iconoclasts for our models. Yet assuredly the great religious problem of modern times is to purge this taint of barbarism away from religion. An attempt has been made here to assert for religion all the sovereign importance that has ever been claimed for it. But all such attempts will be vain and religion will perish in spite of them, if we must needs attribute this sovereign importance to abstract verbal propositions or dogmas. In stationary periods, when but one or two ideas at a time ruffled the mind of nations, such verbal religions might be strong, but not in an age like this, when new ideas come upon us in a torrent that is never intermitted.

We must face once for all the truth that these great views of the Universe upon which states and forms of civilisation rest are partial and provisional, however much they may assert themselves to be final. But we must realise, on the other hand, that states really do rest upon them and not upon nothing at all, so that the decay of a great religion involves a revolution of incalculable magnitude. We are driven then not by some sentimental weakness, but by the feeling that society has claims upon us as well as truth, to the conclusion that in this province New and Old must not be allowed " to meet and clash like armed foes," but that all reasonable means should be tried to graft the new upon the old. This may indeed prove to be impossible. The true view of the Universe must be opened to the population of India, even though it should seem to blot out and cancel all the conceptions in which they have lived for three thousand years. Such is the awful Nemesis of a system which arrests change too long and too successfully! But even there, and much more elsewhere, let what is possible in the way of accommodation be done.

This general view of the nature of religion and of the two great perversions to which it is liable has been applied in this volume to the religious question of the day. We see a great religion approaching the end of its second millennium. It held together for many centuries the civilisation of Europe; it does so to this day more than most suspect. But it suffers from both the perversions.

First, it cannot persuade itself but that all other religions must be its enemies. For a long time it struggled to show that Mohammed must be an impostor, as though the loss of Islam could not but be its own gain. It could not without great effort imagine but that the heathen must be excluded from God's mercy. It was hurt when any strong resemblances to its own creed or scriptures were produced from other sacred books, and has therefore looked on in sheer dismay at the discoveries of recent times, which have shown so much resemblance among most great religions. The curious correspondence, for example, between Buddhism and Christianity affects our religious world with distress, though beforehand one might perhaps have expected it to cause delight and triumph. But such is the nature of religion, which, being an attractive force to those whom it brings together, is a force of violent repulsion towards those who are without.

Secondly, it has allowed itself, like other great religions, to be stereotyped. And it has now entered upon that phase when minds of the higher order are seldom found to receive its ancient dogmas with complete conviction, when they do not altogether belong to it even when they most admire it and most appreciate the service it has rendered to mankind. It has reached this rather advanced stage of decline, and has left quite behind it the first stage when individual disbelievers were indeed numerous enough, but still minds disposed to religion, even when they were minds of the highest order, were troubled with no scepticism that they could not overcome.

This volume has not aimed at combating the scepticism of the age. It has rather assumed that a system of doctrine which has been left unrevised for more than a thousand years must needs provoke scepticism. The only questions here raised have been : How far does the prevalent incredulity extend? and, What course ought to be adopted if its case were completely made good? We have protested against that fatal propensity to exaggerate differences, that taste for discord even when discord is most ruinous, that

craving for excitement which would rather make life a
tragedy than see it deprived of all dramatic interest. We
have argued that not theology as such nor religion as such,
but both only as far as they are founded upon supernaturalism, are attacked by modern philosophy; that undoubtedly an age of progressive discovery cannot regard a
system two thousand years old with the undiscriminating
reverence of the middle age, which looked up in all things
to antiquity as superior to itself; that it will regard the Bible
and the creeds as *archaic* in form; but that on the other
hand it may easily regard them as true in substance or as
presenting grand outlines of truth, since indeed the modern
way of thinking is especially historical and appreciates the
past all the more as it does justice to the future. We have
pointed out analogies between the stern rigour and hatred of
anthropomorphism shown by modern science and the very
same qualities in Hebrew prophecy, between the tone of
Hebrew religion and that nature-worship which breathes in
modern poetry, between the humanity of the modern world
and the spirit of early Christianity; we have remarked, in
short, that both the Old Testament and the New lose that
appearance of obsoleteness which ecclesiastical formalism
has given them, and stand out as true sacred books and
classics of mankind, so soon as in the former Nature is
written for God and in the latter Humanity for Christ.

So much has been urged in respect to the doctrinal
system itself which was established so many centuries ago.
Considered solely in itself it seems to be the archaic outline
of precisely such a religion as would satisfy the modern
world. But secondly we have urged that it would be much

more than this had it not been stereotyped so early, and that the finality which has so long prevailed in religion is peculiarly abusive in the Christian Church and prevents Christianity from doing justice to itself. Other religions have been stereotyped early because their first preachers were narrow-minded and could not conceive of development in religion. But our religion was not at first of this kind, since the most remarkable feature of our Bible is its system of successive revelations covering many centuries, and its doctrine of an Eternal God who from age to age makes new announcements of His will. Here again in archaic form we have a modern doctrine, by the help of which Christianity ought to have been preserved from the fate of other religions which have found themselves incapable of bearing a change of times. It follows that we may find in Christianity itself the principle that may revive Christianity, for the principle of historical development, which is what we need, is plainly there, and the whole Bible is built upon it. Christianity was intended to develop itself, but something arrested it. The spirit of prophecy, that is, of development, did not continue sufficiently vigorous in the Church. It was not indeed absent. The prophet of the Apocalypse and Paul show us in what way Christianity might have faced the new exigencies. In later times too it exhibited itself occasionally. Augustine's *City of God* may be called a true prophecy. The creation of the Papacy is a wonderful proof of life and the power of self-adaptation in the Church. At the Reformation and since true prophets of the ancient type have appeared. And in more recent times outside the Church there has been a disposition to treat the great writer of each period as having a prophetic mission, as though we felt that, the old Hebrew sense of historical development having revived, the Hebrew prophet must revive with it.  But if this spirit had been lively in the Church at all times, if at all periods prophets had been on the watch to discern "the face of the sky and the signs of this time," and the Church had retained the power of receiving a prophet and rendering him due homage, that dangerous gulf which now we witness between the teaching of the Church and the needs of the people need never have opened.

But after all the evil cannot be thought irremediable since the disease is of an ordinary kind and has many times been cured.  This doctrine of development has always been seized with difficulty and soon dropped again ; the prophet, who believes in past and future alike, has always been opposed by those who believe only in the past or only in the future, that is by the majority.  It has been urged here that at least in England and America a reform is still possible, since in both countries the old religion retains its hold not merely upon sentimentalists but upon a vast number of calm and serious minds.

Such a reform must rest upon the principle that as Christianity was wider than Judaism so the religion of the present age must be wider than Christianity, but at the same time as Christianity did not renounce Judaism so our religion must not renounce Christianity.  If the Eternal revealed Himself between Moses and Christ, surely He has not ceased to reveal Himself since the time of Christ  If we say so we cannot be serious, for we *know* that in recent times we have learnt far more of the laws by which the

Universe is governed than former ages knew. Accordingly in this volume an attempt has been made to distinguish the additional element which modern ages have brought but which our stereotyped system has refused to admit or assimilate.

We have noted at what points the human mind seems cramped by the reigning orthodoxy, and so cramped that it cannot permanently submit or acknowledge the wholesomeness of the restraint. We found on the one side artists bitterly complaining of its yoke, of the primness and suspiciousness of its morality; on the opposite side we found science rebelling against the sentimental and unreal view of the Universe which it imposed as dogma and to maintain which it fettered the freedom of inquiry. Both these opposite rebellions appeared to gain strength irresistibly from age to age, and both appeared not irreligious but religious in the spirit that animated them. We could not but acknowledge that the inspiration of the artist though less serious, and that of science though so terribly austere, had the character of religion, that they were binding forces such as destroy selfishness and sustain the Higher Life. Nay, in the latter we seemed to see the very same iconoclastic impulse that lay at the root of Semitic religion, while in the other we found the delicate spirit of Greek Paganism, which had been crushed in the blind rancour of victorious Christianity and had left the world deploring its loss ever since.

Especially of late years and among ourselves Art and Science have proclaimed themselves to be not mere rebels against the reigning religion but rival religions. The change in their tone is very marked. The artist, literary or other, who in Walter Scott's time professed only to furnish amuse-

ment to the public and to be richly contented if they
applauded him, now assumes the air of a priest and makes
it a point of honour to speak of his pursuit as a cult.   The
scientist does this with still more decision; he is now a
priest of Truth as the other of Beauty, and he asks with the
loftiest self-consciousness what any Christian priest can have
to say to him.

According to this volume the Christian priest can only be
silent; it is the penalty he suffers for having allowed himself
to believe that the Eternal, who used in old time to teach
man by successive revelations, has long since ceased to do
so.   But may he not now recover the lost ground by
reviving the Hebrew doctrine of development?

It has been alleged here that he may recover a great part
of it.   For of the new knowledge, the new views of the
Universe, of man, and of the history of man, which have
opened upon us and which make us feel more than ever the
need of spiritual guidance,—though unfortunately they seem
to escape the notice of our authorised spiritual guides; of
this new knowledge by far the larger part is only additional
to our established Christianity and by no means opposed to
it.   The monkish asceticism and horror of nature against
which Art protests, the dread of free inquiry which seems so
contemptible to Science—these are not to be found in the
original Christianity, they are but vices which mark the
failure of Christianity to adapt itself to new and trying
conditions.   There is no reason why Christianity should not
now recognise views of life which are really kindred to its
own, though they were beyond the Hebrew culture of its
first preachers.

But of course in practice there arises a difficulty which cannot long be overlooked and which it has been an object of this volume to deal with. The conception of successive revelations of Himself made by the Eternal, discerned first by prophets, and made by them manifest to all, makes indeed a grand basis for a progressive religion; but how much margin does it allow for mistake? In the Bible itself this conception is handled broadly, and in the style of a nation capable of great ideas, but quite incapable of criticism. There is a remarkably firm grasp of the idea of development in the ages, and of a certain economy in revelation by which it is adapted to the "hardness of heart" of a particular generation. But there is no admission that mistake on a great scale may mix with revelation, that beside the true and the false prophet there may be the mistaken prophet, speaking at one time great truths and at another time falling into great errors. Accordingly we find here no precedent which shall tell us what to do when our religion needs not merely to be developed further, but to be corrected, when it appears not merely unripe but simply mistaken and wrong.

Now such a precedent is just what we need and scarcely know how to do without. For the difficulty which the modern world feels in dealing with its ancient religion is not so much that it has been too much stereotyped—that is a difficulty which might conceivably be surmounted—but that it is mistaken in the most important points. We are told that it needs correcting not developing, and that even this is not the whole truth. Its fundamental statement, upon which avowedly its whole system is built, is itself, it is now maintained, untrue. For what is, what was originally the

R

Gospel, but the announcement that Jesus was risen from the
dead? Now it is the prevalent opinion among those who
are most penetrated with the modern spirit that Jesus did
not rise from the dead. What then can the modern world do
but conclude, however regretfully, in the words of St. Paul
himself, that its faith, the faith of eighteen centuries, is vain?

It is this dilemma which at the present time frustrates
the efforts of those who would hold themselves at liberty to
reject miracle and yet avoid the fathomless abyss which
would be left by the disappearance of the ancient religion of
Christendom. For they are obliged either to pronounce
Christianity a vain faith or to think that St. Paul, speaking
in his most prophetic tone with unusual emphasis and with
an air of the most deliberate solemnity, was mistaken.

But as we suppose development in everything, so we
ought to expect development in the idea of prophecy. The
Hebrews conceived the vision of each prophet to be limited,
so that he would be left behind by the prophet of the next
age. The conception was grand and true, but it would be
absurd that we, with an infinitely larger grasp of history and
with habits of more exact thought, should bind ourselves too
strictly to it. We recognise that there are seers gifted to
trace the course of human destiny, who help us to understand
what new scene in the drama of time is about to open.
But we do not now believe that such seers are merely limited
in their views, we think them capable of error and of great
error. We even think that their intensity is closely connected
with a certain waywardness, and that the very vividness with
which they see some things makes them blind to others; so
that we are never surprised to find them as often more right,

so at times more wrong, than the rest of the world. And whatever we may think either of miracle in general or of the particular miracle of the resurrection, it is difficult now, whether we look at the first rise of Christianity or at its later history, to admit that it hangs by a thread, as St. Paul declares, logically attached to the testimony of Cephas and the Twelve and the Five Hundred. Its basis is rather the whole Judaic conception of the foundation of the state and of the development of history. The grand pages of Hebrew prophecy, including those contained in the Gospels, would not be cancelled if all that testimony were discredited; nay, it is one of the most clearly marked circumstances in the biography of Jesus that the thought of death and resurrection did not rise in His mind till His undertaking had reached an advanced stage. Again it is certain that the other great feature in the history of Christianity, the union it established among European nations and the universal civilisation it thus brought to light, is quite separable in thought from the miracle of the resurrection, however much belief in the miracle may have contributed to bring it about. And this subsequent addition made to Christianity would go far to compensate any loss it might suffer by the loss of its miraculous element.

In a word, Natural Christianity regards prophecy too as natural and therefore highly fallible. It can imagine even St. Paul mistaken. Nevertheless it believes in prophecy, and so far from thinking that no " sure word " is vouchsafed to men, it believes that there not only once were, but that there still are, prophets, or rather vehicles of pure truth concerning man's relation to the Universe and the course of his history far more trustworthy than the Hebrew prophets. It lowers somewhat the value of the ancient Revelation, but it adds a revelation made since and still making.

We conclude, then, that it is a mistake to imagine Christianity as standing or falling with the miracle of the Resurrection, and that it rests, in fact, not on the narrow basis of a disputable occurrence but on the broad foundation of Hebrew religion, Hebrew prophecy, and the historic union of the nations in the Christian Empire. When this is once granted, it will appear that the *unmiraculous* part of the Christian tradition has a value which was long hidden from view by the blaze of supernaturalism. So much will this unmiraculous part gain by being brought for the first time into full light, such new and grand conceptions will arise out of it, illuminating the whole history of mankind, that faith may be disposed to think even that she is well rid of miracle, and that she would be indifferent to it even if she could still believe it. For the religion that thus emerges is in many respects more powerful and animating, mainly because it is more public, than supernatural religion can be. Supernatural religion, all must feel, has not done so much, has not reformed the world so much, as might have been expected. Its failure is evidently due in great part to its supernaturalism, to the unnatural stress it lays upon a future life. To hope even with enthusiastic conviction for a future life is one thing; to be always brooding over it so as to despise the present life in comparison with it is another. The orthodox system is always in practice sliding into this error, because its vision of the future life is far too distinct and mythological. By the side of such a vision everything historical, all the destiny of states and nations, fades away, and men become quietists if not monks. A religion arises which is intensely personal if not selfish, which does not, like the religion of the Bible, accompany history, interpret every historical change, and, in fact, make time, change, and development its subject-matter, but contemplates fixed objects and " forgets itself to marble " in contemplating them.

But as we perceive with great clearness that the original Judaic religion though it had supernaturalism had it not in this form, and instead of being monkish, otherworldly, and immutable was social, political, and historical, we find ourselves reconciled with the past and the future at the same time by pushing the supernaturalism of our religion into the background. By reviving prophecy in its modern form of a philosophy of history we at once adapt religion to the present age and restore it to its original character.

One great object is always before us while we study the Judaic religion in the Bible, Jerusalem or Zion, or the kingdom of God, or the New Jerusalem, or the "city which hath foundations." In the Bible this city, sacred as it is, is exhibited as subject to the vicissitudes of time ; now it is happy and triumphant, now it sits in the dust or is carried into captivity. The supernatural guardianship does not save it from adversity or raise it beyond the reach of sympathy. But in our modern religion this Zion has been transferred across the grave into a starry region of eternal immobility. It is gone away to heaven, which is as much as to say that it is dead. Supernaturalism has killed it.

Now according to the view here presented the spiritual city is here on earth as much as it was in the times of the

Bible. For it is neither more nor less than civilisation itself, which consists not in any visible fabric nor even essentially in institutions, but in religion or worship or the higher life. As in the Bible the spiritual city is identified in language with a definite locality, a visible citadel and temple, and yet is always held separable from such local limitations, so in our view the civilisation of the later world was for a long time gathered into an institution, the great World-Church or World-State of Europe, but yet does not absolutely require such embodiment ; the machinery may grow old and unserviceable ; it may be cast aside, and a time may elapse during which it remains unreplaced. For the spirit, the religion, the worship is not to be identified with any visible forms, so that we are not to be too much astonished if, when the New Jerusalem of modern civilisation appears before us, we "see no temple therein."

This view may fairly claim to be nearer to the original Christian scheme than that which has taken its place. But does it not also supply the link among religious thoughts which is often thought to fail when supernaturalism becomes doubtful ? Without supernaturalism, we are told, religion is mere morality or mere philosophy ; very proper perhaps but mere morality, very true perhaps but mere philosophy ! Not so, for it is inseparably intertwined with politics and history. At the bottom of every state we shall find a religion, a religion underlies universal civilisation, and necessarily therefore religion is the main subject of history.

This view will also be found most useful to the culture of the age. For in our culture there is at present a most dangerous gap. While most other great subjects of know-

ledge have been brought under systematic treatment, rescued
from mere popular misconception, and then, when the
great generalisations have been duly settled, rendered back
to the people in authoritative teaching, one subject remains
an exception, and that one the all-important subject of the
history of civilisation.  No grand trustworthy outlines have
yet been put within the reach of all, which may serve as a
chart to guide us in political and social movement.

Such a chart, it has been pointed out, Hebrew prophecy
in archaic manner gave.  But the work was long ago
broken off, and the result is that history has become for
all popular purposes a chaos.  Who derives guidance from
it?  Who does not lose himself in its labyrinth?  On that
sea we embark without a compass and without any fixed
point by which to steer; we are driven hither and thither
upon it by gusts of national prejudice, or theories taken up
at random.  An abstraction called the State is set up as
a sort of absolute end; its glory or wellbeing made the
standard of public action.  Its relation to other States or to
the whole, the ground of its pretensions, how it arose, why it
exists and whether it will exist for ever, in fact, all the largest
and most urgent questions are decided at random, if they
are decided at all.  On the most important of all subjects
there is put before us a medley of facts unclassified and unverified such as excites the ridicule of the man of science; and
yet we receive them with delighted interest; we are rational
on other subjects but madmen on the greatest subject of all.

This subject, it has been urged, is in the proper sense
theology, and it is the grand topic of the Bible.  Considering man as in the presence of a great Necessity, theology

inquires how his ideals may be conformed to it. The Bible
is a great history of the dealings of a certain human group
with this Necessity, of their attempts to obey it, of their fits
of disobedience and forgetfulness. This is the proper
historical point of view, which must be taken up in modern
history also if it is to become a source of serious instruction,
to have its canonical books, or to cease to be the Babel of
national brawls and mendacious party recriminations that it
is. The remedy lies in regarding history with more reverence,
as a main part of religion; only thus can we save it from
the unprincipled perversion it now suffers at the hands of
party-writers; the remedy lies too in seeing, as the Hebrews
did, not only the struggles of men in history but the decrees
of a superior Necessity, for history is a source of wild
delusions, of the mania of admiration in reactionaries, and
of the frenzy of hatred in revolutionists, to those who see in
it only human free-will.

But what of Supernaturalism? Throughout this volume
it has been held aloof, and our principal object has been to
break the inveterate association which in the general opinion
connects religion with it. We have denied that Supernaturalism is necessary either to the idea, or to the practical
vigour, or to the popular diffusion, of religion. We have
even maintained that when it is made the mainspring of
religion it does harm, since it gives religion an unpractical,
unprogressive character, and withdraws it from the main
current of modern thought. And yet it has been so long
and so uniformly treated by all religious parties as such a
mainspring that when it is removed from this position,

religion is altered and becomes difficult to recognise. It may no doubt produce perplexity when the name of religion is given to that which wants some of the leading characteristics, which, not at some times or in some places only but all over Christendom and from the primitive times of the Church, have been supposed to belong to religion. As described here, religion does not brood over a future life, but is intensely occupied with the present; it does not surmise something behind nature, but contemplates nature itself; it does not worship a Power which suspends natural laws, but the Power which is exhibited in those laws; it does not shrink from political organisation, but is itself the soul of all healthy political organisation; it does not damp enjoyment, but is itself the principle of all rich enjoyment; it is not self-conscious or self-absorbed and does not make us anxious about our own fate, but is the principle which destroys self and gives us strength to rise above personal anxieties. Undoubtedly, if this view be right many medieval saints must have been sadly wrong, and it must be admitted that for long periods strangely foreign elements must have been blended with religion. But after all not much less than this was asserted at the Reformation; after all if we have here deserted the medieval ideal it has been for that of the Hebrew prophets down to the very end of the Hebrew period of religion. For their religion was social, political, historical, and supernaturalism was not the mainspring of it.

But supernaturalism in religion is quite another thing when it is not thus made the mainspring. If we have learnt to see our God in Nature rather than outside Nature it does not follow that we are to regard Him as limited by Nature, that is Nature as known to us. We are all supernaturalists thus far that we all believe in the existence of a world beyond our present knowledge. It is practical Supernaturalism when we allow this world beyond our science to influence us in thought, feeling, or action. We may do so by holding that though we have not science of it yet we have probabilities or powerful presentiments or lastly indications given through exceptional unaccountable occurrences called miracles, which together make its existence practically important to us.

And if we can think so and if the news thus brought to us are good news, who will not say that a supernatural religion, thus supplementing a natural one, may be precious, nay, perhaps indispensable? So much knowledge does our life need, and so little satisfying are the revelations of science, that to many, if not most, of those who feel the need of religion all that has been offered in this book will perhaps at first seem offered in derision. It will be inconceivable to them that religion can be mainly concerned with what all know and all admit. To them religion is only conceivable as a unique solace, or a prop in weakness, or a stay in the eddy, or a substance under the hollowness of life; they do not associate it with happiness, health, or vigour, but exclusively with pain, decay, and death. They think of it as something added to life and knowledge, because life and knowledge fall so dismally short. This view is indeed mischievous so long as it is thus exclusive. It has often been pointed out of late years that Religion loses its old commanding influence when it is thus monopolised by the miserable, that it becomes a melancholy partial thing, a mere makeshift for the science and practical energy which will in the end sweep the world clear of most of our present misery, and make life rich and satisfying through realities not through dreams. To this objection it may be added that we cannot give such an infinite range to our hopes without also heightening our fears, for if we yield too much to the thought that "in a boundless universe there must be boundless better," how can we help feeling at the same time that there must be "boundless worse"? With heaven comes hell, with transcendent hope an unnameable despair. But when this view ceases to be exclusive it acquires quite another character. When the supernatural does not come in to overwhelm the natural and turn life upside down, when it is admitted that religion deals in the first instance with the known and the natural, then we may well begin to doubt whether the known and the natural can suffice for human life. No sooner do we try to think so than pessimism raises its head. The more our thoughts widen and deepen, as the Universe grows upon us and we become accustomed to boundless space and time, the more petrifying is the contrast of our own insignificance, the more contemptible become the pettiness, shortness, fragility of the individual life. A moral paralysis creeps upon us. For a while we comfort ourselves with the notion of self-sacrifice; we say, What matter if I pass, let me think of others! But the *other* has become contemptible no less than the self; all human griefs alike seem little worth assuaging, human happiness too paltry at the best to be worth increasing. The whole moral world is reduced to a point, the spiritual city, "the goal of all the saints" dwindles to the "least of little stars"; good and evil, right and wrong, become infinitesimal, ephemeral matters, while eternity and infinity remain attributes of that only which is outside the realm of morality.   Life becomes more intolerable the more we know and discover, so long as everything widens and deepens except our own duration, and that remains as pitiful as ever.   The affections die away in a world where everything great and enduring is cold ; they die of their own conscious feebleness and bootlessness.

Supernatural Religion met this want by connecting Love and Righteousness with eternity.   If it is shaken how shall its place be supplied?   And what would Natural Religion avail then ?

But still if religion fails us it is only when human life itself is proved to be worthless.   It may be doubtful whether life is worth living, but if religion be what it has been described in this book, the principle by which alone life is redeemed from secularity and animalism,—so that every high thought and liberal sentiment, even if it appear completely divorced from religion, is but a fragment which once had its place in the fabric of some religion and now awaits the time when it can be built in to some new fabric of religion adapted to the coming time,—can it be doubtful that if we are to live at all we must live, and civilisation can only live by religion ?

### THE END

*Printed by* R. & R. CLARK, *Edinburgh.*